NEGEV DESERT

ISRAEL

ISRAEL

By the Editors of Time-Life Books
With photographs by Hans Wiesenhofer

TIME-LIFE BOOKS ∘ ALEXANDRIA, VIRGINIA

TIME® LIFE BOOKS

Other Publications:

MYSTERIES OF THE UNKNOWN
TIME FRAME
FIX IT YOURSELF
FITNESS, HEALTH & NUTRITION
SUCCESSFUL PARENTING
HEALTHY HOME COOKING
UNDERSTANDING COMPUTERS
THE ENCHANTED WORLD
THE KODAK LIBRARY OF
    CREATIVE PHOTOGRAPHY
GREAT MEALS IN MINUTES
THE CIVIL WAR
PLANET EARTH
COLLECTOR'S LIBRARY OF THE CIVIL WAR
THE EPIC OF FLIGHT
THE GOOD COOK
WORLD WAR II
HOME REPAIR AND IMPROVEMENT
THE OLD WEST

This volume is one in a series of books describing countries of the world — their natural resources, peoples, histories, economies and governments.

For information on and a full description of any of the Time-Life Books series listed above, please write:
Reader Information
Time-Life Customer Service
P.O. Box C-32068
Richmond, Virginia 23261-2068
Or call:
1-800-621-7026

Cover: In Jerusalem's Old City, the golden Dome of the Rock — a sacred Islamic shrine — glows above the limestone arcades and apartment blocks of the rebuilt Jewish Quarter. In the background, beyond the turrets of the Roman Catholic Church of the Dormition, new housing developments climb the suburban hills.

Front and back endpapers: A topographic map showing the mountains, deserts and other natural features of Israel appears on the front endpaper; the territories occupied by Israel since 1967 are indicated by a solid line. The back endpaper shows the principal towns, cities and settlements.

Time-Life Books Inc.
is a wholly owned subsidiary of

TIME INCORPORATED

FOUNDER: Henry R. Luce 1898-1967

Editor-in-Chief: Henry Anatole Grunwald
Chairman and Chief Executive Officer: J. Richard Munro
President and Chief Operating Officer: N. J. Nicholas Jr.
Chairman of the Executive Committee: Ralph P. Davidson
Corporate Editor: Ray Cave
Group Vice President, Books: Reginald K. Brack Jr.
Vice President, Books: George Artandi

TIME-LIFE BOOKS INC.

EUROPEAN EDITOR: Kit van Tulleken
Assistant European Editor: Gillian Moore
Design Director: Ed Skyner
Photography Director: Pamela Marke
Chief of Research: Vanessa Kramer
Chief Sub-editor: Ilse Gray

LIBRARY OF NATIONS

Series Editor: Tony Allan

Editorial Staff for *Israel*
Editor: Ellen Galford
Deputy Editor: Christopher Farman
Researcher: Mark Karras
Designer: Mary Staples
Sub-editors: Sally Rowland, Frances Dixon
Picture Department: Christine Hinze, Peggy Tout
Editorial Assistant: Molly Oates

EDITORIAL PRODUCTION

Chief: Jane Hawker
Production Assistants: Nikki Allen, Alan Godwin, Maureen Kelly
Editorial Department: Theresa John, Debra Lelliott

Contributors: The chapter texts were written by Windsor Chorlton, William Frankel, T. R. Fyvel, Marlin Levin and Alan Lothian. Additional material was provided by John Laffin.

Assistant Editor for the U.S. Edition: Barbara Fairchild Quarmby

Pages 1 and 2: Central to the emblem of the state of Israel, shown on page 1, is the Menorah, a seven-branched candlestick commemorating the ancient Temple in Jerusalem. The candelabrum is flanked by two olive branches, linked by the word "Israel" in Hebrew. The nation's blue-and-white flag *(page 2)* is dominated by the Star of David, a six-pointed star that is an age-old symbol first used officially as a Jewish emblem by the Jewish community of Prague in the 1300s. The broad blue bands at the top and bottom of the flag represent the stripes of the prayer shawl traditionally worn by Jewish men during worship.

CONSULTANT

Jon Kimche is the author of many books on Israel and the Middle East. He served for 30 years as the Middle East correspondent for the London *Evening Standard* and has edited a wide range of current-affairs journals and periodicals, including *Tribune, Jewish Observer and Middle East Review, New Middle East* and *Afro-Asian Affairs*.

Special Consultant: Professor P. J. Vatikiotis is Professor of Near and Middle Eastern Politics at the University of London.

PHOTOGRAPHER

Hans Wiesenhofer is an Austrian who has traveled throughout the world on photographic projects. He also works on assignment for a camera maker as a photographer and teacher of photographic techniques. In addition to his assignment on *Israel*, he has contributed photographs to other volumes in the Library of Nations series, including *France, Germany, Italy* and *Australia*.

Second printing. Revised 1987.
Printed in U.S.A.
Published simultaneously in Canada.
School and library distribution by Silver Burdett Company, Morristown, New Jersey.

TIME-LIFE is a trademark of Time Incorporated U.S.A.

Library of Congress Cataloguing in Publication Data
Israel.
    (Library of nations)
    Bibliography: p.
    Includes index.
    1. Israel. 2. Israel — Description and travel — Views. I. Wiesenhofer, Hans, 1954- .
II. Time-Life Books. III. Series.
DS102.95.I86 1987   956.94   86-23176
ISBN 0-8094-5189-1
ISBN 0-8094-5190-5 (lib. bdg.)

CONTENTS

On the outskirts of the sprawling city of Tel Aviv, home to more than one third of Israel's population, an apartment complex rises above a development of solar-heated houses. Eighty-five percent of Israelis live in the country's densely settled towns and cities.

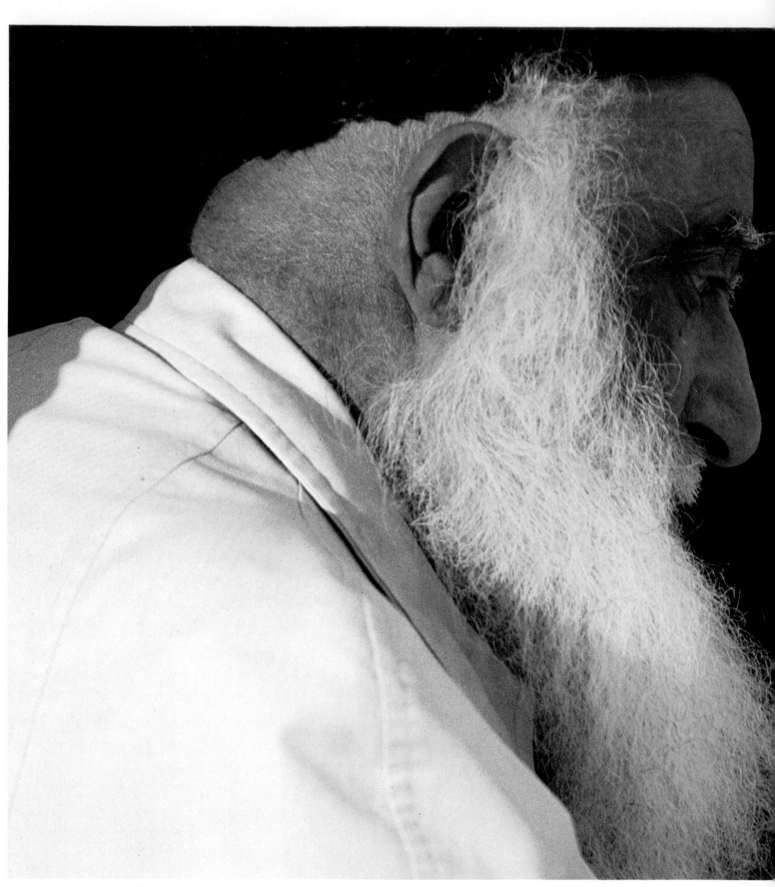

An elderly Jewish man studies a text in Hebrew, a language written from right to left with an alphabet of 22 letters. Unlike other modern languages, which

REBIRTH OF AN ANCIENT LANGUAGE

The official language of Israel is Hebrew, a modern tongue with an ancient pedigree. Spoken by Jewish people until the third century B.C., when most of the Old Testament was written, Biblical Hebrew gradually lost ground to the languages of Palestine's conquerors: the Persians, Greeks and Romans. Hebrew survived into the 19th century only as an instrument of rabbinical study and religious ritual, its concepts and vocabulary anchoring it firmly in the world of Abraham and Moses.

In 1880, a Lithuanian Zionist named Eleizer Ben-Yehuda realized that Jews returning to Palestine needed their own language, "a language in which we can conduct the business of life." He singlehandedly began the massive task of building the Old Testament vocabulary of only 7,704 words into a contemporary vernacular. Scouring ancient texts for Hebrew roots, he adapted them to fit modern meanings. Appropriately, his first word was *millon,* or "dictionary," because his life's work was the completion of the first four books of a 17-volume Hebrew lexicon — the foundation of a language that now includes some 50,000 words.

Although many purists attacked him for debasing the language of worship, Ben-Yehuda succeeded. Today, Hebrew is the vernacular for 83 percent of Israel's Jewish population.

were spoken before they were written, contemporary Hebrew is the only colloquial tongue derived from a written language.

VARIED CLIMATES IN A SMALL LAND

For so small a country — only 8,300 square miles — Israel displays dramatic variations in climate. The coastal plain and inland mountains around Jerusalem have similar climates: hot, dry summers and mild, humid winters. But the mountains are wetter and colder than the plain, and they sometimes have snow. The steppes have a drier climate, supporting dwarf shrubs, grasses and cereals, giving way to semidesert in the northern Negev, where some crops are irrigated. Israel's southern region is extreme desert, a stony and inhospitable area where temperatures can reach 113° F.

MEDITERRANEAN

STEPPE

DESERT

EXTREME DESERT

Haifa

Tel Aviv

Jerusalem

Beersheba

Eilat

Overlooked by the brooding Negev Hills, a straggling herd of domesticated Arabian camels plods the stony landscape of the desert in search of edible

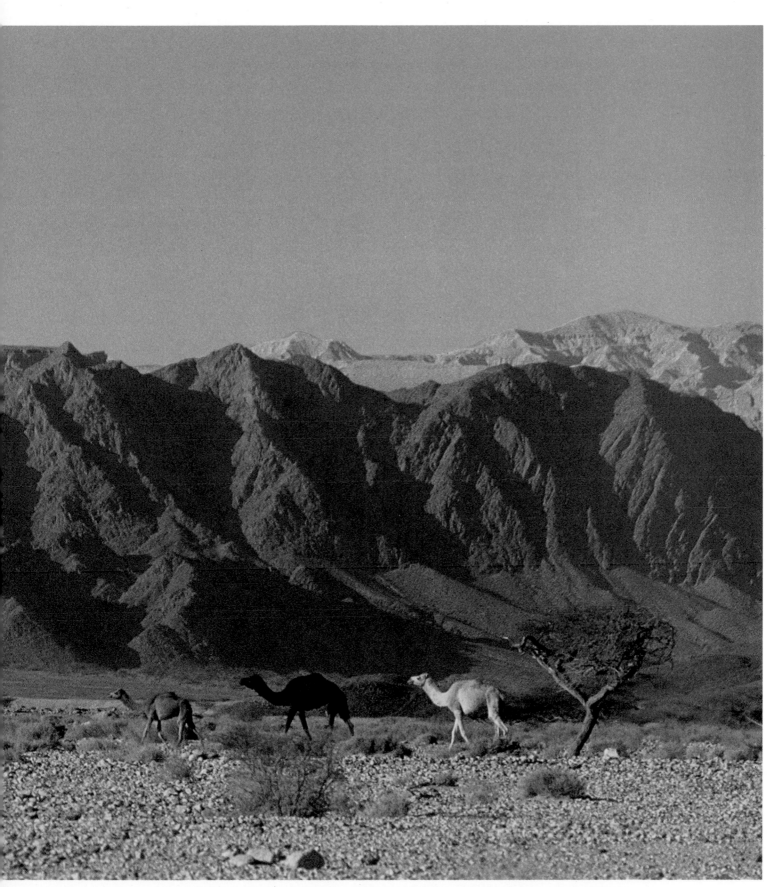

vegetation. Camels are superbly adapted to life in arid regions, storing fat in their humps for nourishment when food is scarce.

WHERE FAITHS CONVERGE

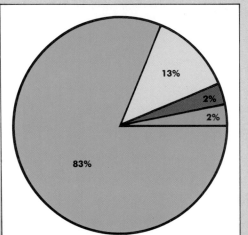

Virtually all Israelis belong to one of the religious groups recognized by the state — Jewish, Muslim, Christian and Druze — with Jews in the majority at 83 percent of the population. Since the days when the Ottoman Turks ruled Palestine, each religious community has kept its autonomous ecclesiastical courts, which rule on matters of marriage, divorce and inheritance. On behalf of all the religions, the state protects the many holy sites within its boundaries, guaranteeing access for all Israeli worshippers, as well as for pilgrims from around the world.

JEWISH

CHRISTIAN

MUSLIM

DRUZE

Raised by the Caliph of Damascus in 691 A.D., Jerusalem's gold-capped Dome of the Rock marks the stony outcropping from which Muhammad leaped to heaven astride his miraculous horse. The rock is also sacred in Judeo-Christian tradition, as the site of Abraham's intended sacrifice of his son Isaac.

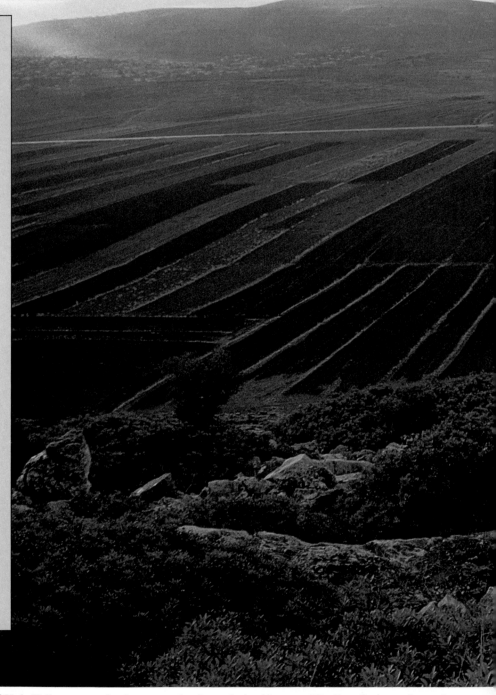

RECLAIMING A WASTELAND

Transformed in just four decades from hostile desert and swamp to richly productive fields and orchards, Israel's farmland is a showpiece of modern agricultural technology. The country's drive to increase food production during a flood of immigration in the 1950s brought mechanization, chemical fertilizers and pesticides — as well as improved strains of livestock and crops — to small farming settlements throughout Israel. In 1949, farmers were irrigating about 75,000 acres; by the 1980s, almost 550,000 acres were being irrigated, producing two or more harvests a year in some areas.

Although widespread irrigation revolutionized agriculture in Israel's arid zone, not all of the 1.1 million acres brought under cultivation since 1930 have been reclaimed from desert. In 1951, engineers began a seven-year project to drain Lake Hula and its surrounding swamp, 25 square miles of malarial wasteland in Upper Galilee. By altering the course of the Jordan River and constructing a network of canals, they created the country's most fertile land.

Today, Israeli agriculture, which employs about 82,000 people, is entirely self-sufficient in the production of vegetables, fruit, milk, eggs and poultry. Israel's exports range from cotton to carnations, in addition to the citrus fruits it has always marketed abroad. Israel also exports its expertise in agricultural development. Thousands of Israeli agronomists have served as consultants for irrigation and desert-farming projects around the world.

A patchwork of ripening crops spreads across the broad Hula Valley, a once-desolate swampland now drained by some 25 miles of man-made canals.

Planted in cotton, grain, peanuts and fruit trees, the valley is also the site of approximately one half of Israel's fresh-water fish ponds.

1

A STATE BORN IN STRIFE

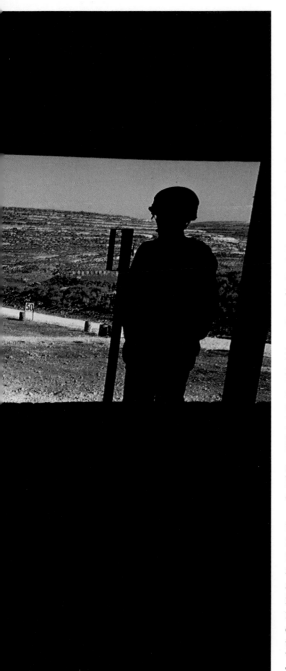

Silhouetted against a sun-baked rifle range, three soldiers prepare to test their marksmanship with high-powered rifles. National defense is the highest priority of the Israeli government, accounting for more than one quarter of its annual budget.

At 4 o'clock in the afternoon on Friday May 14, 1948, shortly before the onset of the Sabbath, 200 leaders of Palestine's Jewish community gathered in the Tel Aviv Museum. After the Palestine Symphony Orchestra had played the Zionist anthem "Hatikvah" ("The Hope"), David Ben-Gurion rose and read a short declaration announcing the establishment of the independent state of Israel. Twelve hours later, as the sun rose over the newborn nation, the armies of Syria, Iraq, Trans-Jordan and Egypt invaded.

Egyptian Spitfires roared over the rooftops of Tel Aviv. Radio audiences listening to a live Independence Day broadcast from Ben-Gurion could hear the thunder of bombs exploding over the outskirts of the city as he spoke. From Cairo, Azzam Pasha, secretary general of the Arab League warned: "This will be a war of extermination and a momentous massacre, which will be spoken of like the Mongolian massacres and the Crusades."

Few outside Israel doubted him. Although the opposing forces were roughly equal in number, the Arab armies were well-equipped with modern artillery and armor, supplied by Britain and France, while the Israelis were relying on 3-inch British and American mortars left over from World War II, old French 65-mm. howitzers of the type used in the 1870 Franco-Prussian War, and kibbutz-made armored cars. The Syrians advanced into Upper Gali-

lee, the Iraqis crossed the coastal plain to a point less than 10 miles from the sea, threatening to split Israel in two, and the Trans-Jordanian Arab Legion laid siege to Jerusalem, capturing the Old City, including the Jewish quarter, on May 25. In the south, one Egyptian thrust came within 20 miles of Tel Aviv, while another approached Jerusalem from the south.

But the Israelis, better trained than their enemies and fighting for their very existence, weathered the initial attacks. Gradually, they took the offensive, recapturing all the territory lost in the first few weeks, except for the Old City of Jerusalem. As fighting continued, they took new territory, in Galilee, Judaea and the Negev, where only the Gaza Strip, bordering the Sinai peninsula, remained in Arab hands. The war, interrupted by truces and cease-fires, continued until July 1949, when Syria signed an armistice agreement with Israel. Altogether the war cost the 600,000-strong Jewish population some 6,000 lives; the Egyptian forces lost 1,500 men, while the casualties of other Arab states are not known.

Both sides believed their cause was just. The Jews were fighting to establish an independent state in Palestine, the narrow strip of the eastern Mediterranean coast that had been the home of their ancestors in Biblical times. For nearly 2,000 years, they had been a scattered, persecuted people, who kept the memory of their homeland alive in

1

their prayers and psalms: "If I forget thee, O Jerusalem: let my right hand forget her cunning."

This longing for Zion — the ancient name for the lost holy city — became one of the bonds that kept the Jews together in the Diaspora. Then, late in the 19th century, there emerged a movement of Jewish nationalists — Zionists — who sought to end the long exile and return to Palestine.

But the Arabs of the Middle East questioned this claim. Jews, they said, may have occupied the place in ages past, but Arabs had lived continuously on the land since the seventh century A.D. (Indeed, according to some Arab historians, their ancestors were the original Semitic inhabitants whom the wandering Israelites supplanted.) The local Arabs themselves were never the sovereign power — Palestine had been annexed by one foreign power after another — but they had eked a living, however precarious, from the stony soil. By the beginning of the 20th century, the Arab communities throughout the Middle East were growing restive under the domination of the Ottoman Turkish Empire, and they were gradually beginning to develop their own nationalist movements.

Inevitably, the conflicting interests and aspirations of the Arabs and the growing numbers of Zionist settlers led to strife: As the 20th century progressed, Palestine increasingly became one of the world's trouble spots. With words as well as weapons, Arabs and Jews fought over territorial rights, sowing seeds of bitterness that continue to bear fruit today.

By the 1930s, the need for a homeland was no longer only a matter of idealism, but a question of survival: Germany produced Hitler and brought forth the Nazi program for the extermination of the Jews. And while the Arabs may have watched this tragedy unfolding in Europe, they stiffened their resistance to the Zionist threat.

After the defeat of Germany, when the refugee camps in Europe were overflowing with 300,000 homeless survivors of the Holocaust, the newly founded United Nations proposed a solution to the conflict: a partition of Palestine into separate Jewish and Arab states. Jerusalem would be designated an international city, freely accessible to the adherents of all faiths. The proposal to internationalize the city was rejected by King Abdullah of Jordan, who occupied the Arab part of the city, and by the Jews.

Nevertheless, in November 1947, the United Nations General Assembly voted for partition, giving the Jews control of 5,500 square miles of the land and giving the Arabs 4,500 square miles.

On this particular issue, the United States and the Soviet Union were, for once, in accord: The establishment of an independent Jewish state in the strategically vital Middle East suited both nations' political interests, and both gave their blessing.

As a result, the birth of the new country was greeted simultaneously by a fund of international good will and by implacable Arab hostility. The Arab nations regarded the mass immigration of Jews into the new state as one more manifestation of European colonialism. They felt that the Western nations and the Soviet Union were using the establishment of Israel as a method of solving Europe's postwar Jewish refugee problem — and as a way of assuaging Europe's collective post-Holocaust guilt — at the expense of the Arabs.

About 450,000 Palestinian Arabs had left the country as a result of the establishment of the Israeli state in May 1948. They sought refuge in Syria, Jordan, Lebanon and in the Gaza Strip.

Any opportunities that had arisen for the Jews and Arabs to work out some form of peaceful coexistence had been missed or mishandled by all parties. The needs and aspirations of the two peoples appeared irreconcilable.

Indeed, the emergence of a Jewish nation had a revolutionary impact on the Arab world. In Egypt — then Israel's principal and most powerful Arab adversary — the resulting tremors led to the overthrow of King Farouk in 1952. The new regime of "Free Officers," headed by Gamal Abdel Nasser, promoted a militant Egyptian-directed Arab nationalism that sought to confront and constrain the emergent Jewish state. The hostility culminated in the Sinai Campaign of 1956, when Israeli forces defeated the Egyptians in the barren peninsula between southern Israel and the Suez Canal, achieving victory after barely 100 hours of combat. Israel held the peninsula for six

months, then withdrew after securing a United Nations pledge to guard the Gaza Strip. In addition, the Egyptians undertook to allow Israeli ships passage through the Gulf of Aqaba from Israel's new port of Eilat.

Ten years later, in June 1967, the Egyptians, along with Jordan and Syria, again sought to gain the upper hand and set up a blockade against Israel in the Gulf of Aqaba. But, in a series of surprise maneuvers that has been described as one of the swiftest and most shattering feats of arms in history, the Israelis were able to destroy the opposing air and ground strength in a war lasting only six days.

In this clash, Israel retook the Sinai and also acquired the Gaza Strip and the Golan Heights — the strategically important highlands between Israel and Syria. More significant was Israel's occupation of Arab territories on the West Bank — the 30-mile-wide band of territory between Israel's 1949 eastern boundary and the Jordan River, including East Jerusalem and the Old City. For all Jews, the taking of the Old City after savage hand-to-hand fighting was the greatest triumph of the war,

since it gave them access to the Western Wall, a remnant of the Second Temple and the most sacred shrine of the Jews, from which they had been barred by the Jordanians since 1948.

This time the Israelis did not hand back the spoils of war. In lieu of a final peace settlement and negotiations with the Arabs for recognized and secure boundaries, the armistice boundaries of 1949 were swept away and all the occupied areas were placed under Israeli military administration.

It was the Israelis who were taken by surprise in 1973. The Egyptians invaded the Sinai on Yom Kippur, Judaism's holiest day, reclaiming a narrow strip of the Suez fringe territory lost in the Six Day War, before they were halted by Israeli counterattacks; the fighting spilled over to the Egyptian mainland.

The Egyptians' initial success, however, helped to restore their self-confidence, making it easier for them to negotiate a peace treaty with Israel. This agreement — in which U.S. President Carter played a major role and for which Israel's Prime Minister Begin and Egypt's President Sadat were jointly awarded the Nobel Peace Prize in

The mosques and minarets of Acre's Old City overlook the harbor — the busiest in the Holy Land until 19th-century commercial shipping outgrew it. Once a strategic prize for invading Greeks, Romans and Crusaders, Acre now is home to a small fishing fleet.

Peeping over a Bedouin veil, smiling beneath a chic European hair style, gazing benignly above Christian vestments — the faces of Israel are a vivid mosaic of diverse peoples. The various Semitic groups native to the Holy Land, from nomadic desert tribes to communities of Druze, live side by side with newcomers from all the lands where Jews were scattered. The resettlement of entire towns from places as far-flung as Yemen, Bulgaria, Iraq, Morocco and India has kept ethnic identities alive, but Israeli nationality is a common bond. Today, blue-eyed children whose Polish grandparents fled the Nazis in the 1930s share citizenship with black Jews from Ethiopia, Bahais of Persian descent, Palestine Arabs and Armenians.

1

1978—was signed in March 1979 and successfully implemented in April 1982, when Israel turned the Sinai over to Egypt. The withdrawal met with bitter opposition in some Israeli quarters—particularly among military officers who felt that the desert should be retained as a defense buffer against any future attack from the south, and among the Jewish settlers who in some cases had to be evicted by force from the lush settlement they had cultivated in the Sinai desert soil.

This new Israeli-Egyptian accord was rejected by most other Arab states, and by the Palestinian nationalist movement, whose main military and political wing, the Palestine Liberation Organization (PLO), continued to attack targets in Israel from bases inside Lebanon. On June 6, 1982, a large Israeli armored force crossed the northern border in an invasion designated Operation *Peace for Galilee,* a campaign designed to eliminate the PLO presence in Lebanon. The Israeli bombing of Beirut and the capture of many PLO positions eventually led to the evacuation, by land and by sea, of some 8,000 PLO personnel. Yet the war continued against Syrian forces and Lebanese Muslim guerrillas into 1986, with losses on both sides escalating even as Israeli troops withdrew.

Despite much bloodshed, Israel and its neighbors have not achieved a lasting, formal peace. The nation's boundaries remain in dispute, and Israel's very right to exist as a sovereign state has not yet been officially acknowledged by most Arab governments.

So it is that an Israeli who came young to the Promised Land may have seen combat in five wars in less than four decades. Moreover, some Israelis have fought two or three times for the same strategic point. And the battlegrounds are never more than a few hours' drive from home. In such a small nation, the names recorded on the casualty lists are often those of friends or relatives. "The secret of this country," a Haifa doctor once observed, "is that there is no unknown soldier."

Inevitably, the conflicts have made their impact on the Israeli character. On the one hand, their feats of arms have given Israelis a sense of self-confidence and competence, a feeling that the long roll call of martyrs from the days when the Jews were a persecuted, subject people is a thing of the past. On the other hand, decades of encirclement by hostile Arab neighbors have bred a claustrophobic sense of isolation, a seeming indifference to affairs outside their own region and an apparent cynicism about the motives of other countries—even friendly ones. Israelis know they are the focus of considerable world attention—only Washington, D.C., and Paris host a larger foreign press corps than Jerusalem—and Israelis often feel they are judged by a harsher standard than their adversaries. Yet no outside observer can be more critical of Israel than the Israelis themselves. The invasion of Lebanon, for example, stimulated a ground swell of dissent: Many citizens questioned the validity of the war. And the establishment of Jewish settlements on the West Bank has been as contentious an issue within Israel as it has been outside.

And, in times of crisis, the mood in Israel can swing violently between euphoria and depression, depending on the news reports. Israelis are avid listeners to news broadcasts, for they know that, in the political maelstrom of the Middle East, their country's fortunes may change between one news bulletin and the next. In battle, they listen to the news even as they make it: An estimated 70 percent of combat soldiers in the Six Day War took their radios with them to the front.

In a country so often on the firing line, it is not surprising that there should be a conspicuous military presence. With the exception of ultra-orthodox Jews, the medically exempt and the Arab minority, all Israelis must serve in the Zahal, the country's unified defense forces. Men are mobilized at the age of 18 for three years, and until they are 40, they must report for 31 days' training annually; thereafter, until the age of 55, they must serve 14 days a year. Women, who serve as drivers, instructors and communications personnel but not as front-line combatants, are drafted for two years and are liable for the reserves until they reach the age of 34 or have a child. There is truth in the remark that an Israeli is a soldier with 10 months' annual leave.

In Israel, the military is everywhere. At every major highway intersection, there are lines of armed, hitchhiking soldiers; road blocks guard the approaches to sensitive Arab areas; and armed sentries patrol the barbed-wire fences that surround almost all of the more isolated settlements.

On the Golan Heights, the sense of a country under siege is oppressively strong. Roads are corrugated by tank tracks; directional signs are riddled with bullet holes made, apparently, by advancing Syrian troops; yellow posts every 100 yards mark the entrance to bomb shelters. In some places, burned-out tanks and wrecked personnel carriers remain—fossils of past conflicts. Buzzards perch on abandoned, shellshattered Arab villages; gazelles step daintily across mine fields. White-painted United Nations vehicles driven by cease-fire observers bump down tracks to their heavily fortified bases. On the treeless, gently undulating land, nothing moves without being seen and tracked. The commanding heights bristle with gun emplacements, listening devices, radar scanners. The air seems to hum with radio traffic.

To a traveler from a country at peace, these sights and sounds may seem sinister, but to many Israelis, they are a constant reassurance. In the border areas, the military presence has been accepted as a grim necessity.

For all its military gains, Israel remains a very small country. Its total area within the 1949 armistice lines is only about 8,000 square miles, which makes it roughly the same size as the state of New Jersey or, as some Israelis point out, less than 1 percent of the area of its Arab neighbors. From the Lebanese border to the Sinai, Israel is 260 miles long; in breadth, it ranges from 72 miles at its widest to less than 13. Occupied areas of the Golan Heights, the West Bank and the Gaza Strip add another 2,673 square miles.

To a visitor, Israel seems much bigger than it is. The reason lies in the incredible diversity of its landscapes, which confer a sense of space that much larger countries sometimes lack. Beyond the heavily urbanized and relatively undifferentiated coastal plain, the most disparate of features — mountain, desert, forest and steppe — are sometimes separated by only a couple of miles. Writers of tourist brochures are fond of claiming that, in the course of a single day in winter, it is possible to take an early-morning run on the ski

AN AGE-OLD DREAM COME TRUE

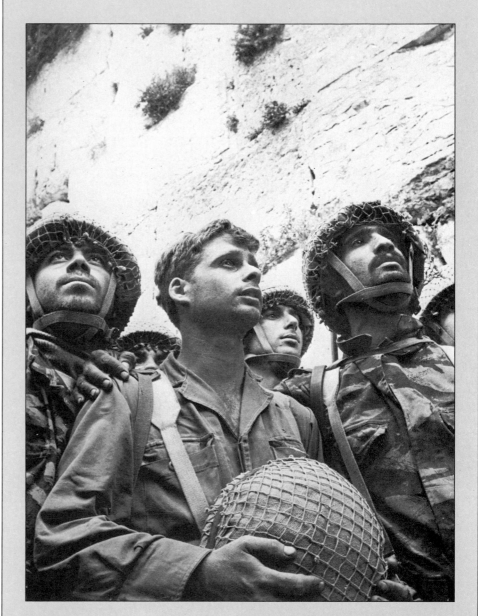

Flanked by troops who have just helped rout the Jordanians from East Jerusalem, a young Israeli soldier doffs his helmet at the Western (Wailing) Wall on the morning of June 7, 1967 — the third day of the so-called Six Day War, in which Israel defeated the forces of Egypt, Syria and Jordan. The solemn expressions reflect the awe Jews felt at the sight of their holiest shrine, cut off for 18 years by the trenches, barbed wire and battlements that had divided the city since Israel's foundation in 1948. Eyewitness and future prime minister Itzhak Rabin described liberation's effect on battle-hardened soldiers: "Their eyes were moist with tears, their speech incoherent. The overwhelming desire was to touch the Wall."

slopes of Mount Hermon in the north and then drive south in time for an evening swim among coral reefs and tropical fish in the Red Sea at Eilat. On the way, a tourist would pass through the subtropical Jordan Valley, lush with date palms and banana groves, drop down into the valley of the Dead Sea, the lowest point on the earth's surface, and cross the wastes of the Negev Desert, parts of which receive less than three quarters of an inch of rain a year.

Given the condition of Israel's roads — adequate, but hardly expressways — a safer proposal would be to take a week for the journey, which would allow time to see the fertile valleys and the forested hills of Galilee, the rolling steppelands of Samaria and the semi-arid badlands of Judaea.

The variety of Israel's landscapes is related both to the country's abrupt changes of topography and to the fact that it lies in a transitional zone between a Mediterranean and a desert climate and is located at the crossroads of Asia, Africa and Europe. All these factors combine to give Israel a range of plant and animal life that is extraordinarily rich and varied. More than 3,000 plants and about 80 species of mammals — including hyenas, jackals, desert wolves and wild boar — have been identified. In terms of its natural history, Israel is a microcosm of three continents.

For different reasons, the same can be said of its human population. By virtue of its location on the cusp of Africa and Asia, at a point where ancient trade routes converge, Israel has always been a meeting place for different tribes and races, but the country's current mix of populations only began to take shape after the birth of the state, when Israel's doors were dramatically opened to Jewish immigrants from all over the world.

At the beginning of 1948, when Independence was declared, the Jewish population of Palestine was estimated to be 600,000. The non-Jewish population for the whole of Palestine on the eve of the War of Independence was about 1.8 million. The war dramatically changed the demographic balance. The mainly Arab areas of Palestine — the West Bank and Gaza Strip, with an Arab population of more than one million — were annexed by Jordan and Egypt respectively. By 1951, the Jewish state of Israel had a Jewish population that had increased threefold in the three years since independence. The Arab population of Israel, which now excluded the West Bank and Gaza, had shrunk to 165,000.

The Declaration of Independence had stated that Israel "will be open to the immigration of Jews from all countries of their dispersion," and during the war itself, 119,000 arrived, some of them becoming Israeli citizens and casualties of war on the same day. Most of the early immigrants were survivors of the Holocaust, but after the war, which jeopardized the safety of Jews living in Arab countries, an increasing number of immigrants came from North Africa and the Middle East.

In 1950, for example, the entire community of 50,000 Yemeni Jews was transferred to Israel by the airborne Operation *Magic Carpet,* and in the following year, the entire Iraqi Jewish community — some 150,000 people — was brought to Israel.

Israel's total population is now about 4.3 million. This figure does not include the people without Israeli citizen-

BORDERS CHANGED BY WAR

In 1947, the United Nations ratified the creation of a Jewish state out of part of Palestine. Since then, successive wars have changed the boundaries of Israel. The 1949 borders marked the battle lines at the end of Israel's War of Independence with neighboring Arab states. The 1967 Six Day War brought the Sinai peninsula, the Gaza Strip, the West Bank, East Jerusalem and the Golan Heights under Israeli control. The 1973 war with Egypt and Syria ended in Israel's withdrawal from the western bank of the Suez Canal. Israel held captured Syrian territory east of the Golan Heights until 1974, however, when the United Nations made the area a demilitarized zone. In 1979, a treaty with Egypt led to Israel's gradual withdrawal from Sinai.

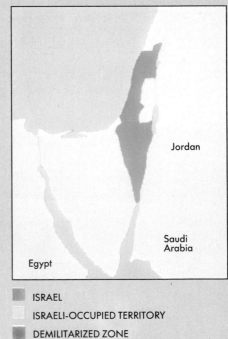

1949

Jordan

Saudi Arabia

Egypt

■ ISRAEL

☐ ISRAELI-OCCUPIED TERRITORY

■ DEMILITARIZED ZONE

ship — almost all Arabs — living in the occupied zones. Eighty-three percent of Israeli citizens are Jews, of whom about 60 percent were born in the country, 22 percent were born in Europe (including the Soviet Union), the Americas or Australasia, and 10 percent were born in North Africa.

During 2,000 years of the Diaspora, several different Jewish communities have emerged, each reflecting the cultural and linguistic customs of the countries in which they lived. By tradition, the Jews fall into two main groups — the Ashkenazim and the Sephardim. The Ashkenazim have their roots in central and eastern Europe, where they spoke Yiddish or German. The Sephardim trace their origins to the culturally and materially rich Jewish community that lived in Spain until

the end of the 15th century; they spoke a Spanish dialect called Ladino. In the 18th century, descendants of the Spanish Jews arrived in Palestine, where they established a center of Jewish mysticism in the northern town of Safed. Today, the Sephardim and the Oriental Jews of North Africa and the Middle East who speak Hebrew with the same accent and follow similar religious rites, are classed together as a single religious and cultural community.

For 60 percent of Israel's population, the first language is Hebrew — a language that had been preserved primarily for liturgical and literary purposes during the Jews' two millennia of wandering. But toward the end of the 19th century, Zionists began to adapt it for modern life in their hoped-for homeland, altering the original alphabet

and vastly expanding the vocabulary.

Arabic is Israel's second official language, spoken not only by Arabs but by a growing number of Jews, and English is the lingua franca and a compulsory subject at school: All three languages appear on many road signs. Although Hebrew is now the dominant form of communication, the babel of languages resulting from large-scale immigration has not yet died out. Of the 23 daily local newspapers on sale in Israel in the mid-1980s, only 11 were in Hebrew, with 12 of them published in Arabic, English, French, Bulgarian, Hungarian or other languages.

Most of Israel's Muslims — like most of the Arab population in the Middle East — belong to the Sunni sect. In religious matters they enjoy virtual auton-

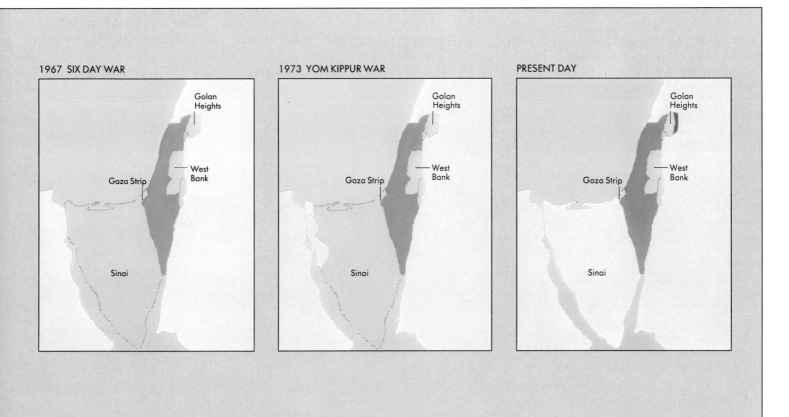

1967 SIX DAY WAR

1973 YOM KIPPUR WAR

PRESENT DAY

Golan Heights

Gaza Strip

West Bank

Sinai

1

omy, and officially they enjoy the same civic freedoms and rights as Jewish citizens of the state. They are, however, exempt from military service — not because they are under any cloud of suspicion, say Israeli authorities, but in recognition of the impossible situation that would confront them if asked to do battle against their coreligionists.

Most of the Arabs in Israel live in Galilee, in Nazareth or in the Haifa and Jerusalem areas, and they work in the cities, where they are joined by about 35,000 workers who commute daily from the Gaza Strip. But approximately 40,000 Arabs, who are members of 23 Bedouin tribes, live in the Negev, where some of them still practice a nomadic way of life.

The Muslim population also includes about 2,500 Circassians: Sunni Muslims who came to Palestine, parts of Trans-Jordan and Syria in the 1870s, when their homeland in the Caucasus region of Russia was occupied by tsarist Christians. In Israel they live in two villages in Galilee.

The Druze, of whom there were about 47,000 in the 1980s, form another religious community, with its own spiritual leadership and religious courts of law. They are the followers of a sect that grew out of Islam in the early 11th century. In the War of Independence, the Druze chose to remain in Israel, and since 1957, the Druze youth have done military service in the Israeli Defense Forces.

About 14 percent of the non-Jewish population in Israel is Christian; the Christians are mostly Arabic-speaking and were born in the country. Greek Catholics account for 40 percent of the total and Greek Orthodox for another 30 percent or more, but in all at least 30 denominations are represented, including members of the Coptic, Syrian Orthodox, Armenian Orthodox, Roman Catholic and Ethiopian churches, as well as various Protestant sects.

For Muslims, Christians and Jews alike, the land of Israel is holy ground: The place names are familiar throughout the world. In the north are the hills of Galilee, bounded in the east by the Jordan River. Their slopes merge with the highlands of Samaria, the ancient center of the Samaritan sect and today a center of militant Palestine Arab nationalism. Looking south from the hills of Jerusalem, halfway down the length of Israel, is Bethlehem, birthplace of Jesus; looking southeast is the wilderness of Judaea, where John the Baptist preached repentance and promised that "the Kingdom of Heaven is at hand." Where the Judaean hills end in the south, the Negev begins; it is here — where modern Israelis are reclaiming the desert — that the three Old Testament patriarchs, Abraham, Isaac and Jacob, pastured their flocks near the town of Beersheba.

So much history saturates the land that whenever a ditch is dug or the foundations for a building excavated, the shovels are likely to bring up relics of long-vanished eras. Israelis are profoundly conscious of the past; indeed, they are obsessed with recovering evidence of it, as if digging down through strata of civilization's debris will put them back in touch with their origins. In Israel, archeology is not only an important university discipline, it is also a national pastime — one that receives the kind of media coverage that other countries usually accord to sports.

It would be wrong, however, to think that the Israelis preserve their land as some kind of museum. The face of modern Israel is conspicuously new — disappointingly utilitarian, perhaps, for visitors whose imagination has been colored by centuries of paintings depicting Biblical scenes against a background of idealized landscapes. But many Israelis would defend themselves against criticism by replying that they have had no time for romanticism: They have been far too busy fighting for their lives with one hand while building a country with the other.

When David Ben-Gurion, Israel's first prime minister, arrived in Palestine in 1906, the coastal plain he had to cross on his way to Jerusalem was largely a wilderness, its rivers lost in malarial swamps, its ancient cities in collapse and invaded by drifting sand dunes, its soil choked with weeds. A few decades later, the coastal strip between Haifa and Gaza has become Israel's most populous and intensively cultivated region, with every piece of ground outside the cities given over to citrus groves, orchards, vineyards, cotton plantations and vegetable gardens.

With its regimented groves of orange trees and their associated canneries, its acres of vegetables shrouded in plastic sheeting and its bleak concrete dairies and chicken farms, the area is not exactly a rural idyll, but it is certainly productive. In spite of a nearly sixfold population increase since 1948, by the mid-1980s the country was self-sufficient in vegetables, citrus and subtropical fruits, milk and eggs.

The foundation of Israeli agriculture was established by Zionist pioneers, who fervently believed that the salvation of the Jews was to be found in the earth. The key to agriculture's present success, however, has been the introduction of new crops, new methods and, above all, the efficient develop-

1

ment of the country's meager water resources. In Israel, almost all rain falls in winter, and the average annual rainfall drops from 28 inches in the north to less than eight inches throughout the southern half of the country. Of the more than one million acres under cultivation in the middle of the 1980s, half were watered artificially. Some of this water came from deep wells on the spot, but most had its source in the Jordan Rift Valley. The Jordan River may still be sacred and eternal, but only in memory. To the Israelis it is a necessary resource to be diverted, channeled, piped, made to flow uphill and generally exploited for the good of the nation.

At some points along its 200-mile-long course, the Jordan is scarcely more than a narrow, ambling stream, but south of the fertile Hula Valley, reclaimed from swampland, the Jordan justifies its name, which means "down rusher," by dropping 885 feet in nine

On a wildlife reserve in the Negev, where conservationists are attempting to reestablish the flora and fauna native to the ancient Holy Land, a herd of rare scimitar-horned oryx rest beneath a shady acacia tree. Israel has some 180 nature preserves.

miles before entering the Sea of Galilee. This sea — technically a lake — is called Yam Kinneret in Hebrew because, seen from afar, it resembles a *kinnor,* or harp. At 700 feet below sea level, it is the lowest body of fresh water in the world. "Fresh" is something of an exaggeration, however: Mineral springs, which can be seen erupting at various parts of the lake, make it noticeably saline. To Christians, it is a site of sacred memory. Here, Jesus walked on the waters; here, he gathered together his disciples Simon, Andrew, James and John. And despite the changes that have been wrought — the concrete and glass hotels of Tiberias, the waterfront restaurants selling St. Peter's fish and soft drinks, the sailboards skimming the surface — it is a place that still evokes its Biblical past.

With an area of 64 square miles and a maximum depth of 150 feet, it is also Israel's largest reservoir, containing nearly twice as much fresh water as Israel consumes in a single year. Unfortunately, the Sea of Galilee is in the wrong place: It not only lies well below most of the cultivated land in the country but is cut off from the parched south by the Judaean highlands.

But, with no other suitable source of water available, the Israelis have had to use the Sea of Galilee as the source of the National Water Carrier, a massive development project that was completed in 1964. From the northwestern corner of the lake, water is pumped to a height of 840 feet, and then it flows through a 10-mile-long canal to another pumping station, which in turn raises it 482 feet above sea level. The water is next conducted through a series of giant pipes, aqueducts, tunnels, reservoirs and dams, which take it, at its farthest terminus, a distance of 88.5 miles across the hills of Galilee, down the coastal plain, and into the northern Negev southwest of Beersheba.

For Prime Minister Ben-Gurion, the completion of the project, which increased the water supply to the Negev by 75 percent, was a major step toward the fulfillment of a long-cherished dream to make the desert bloom. The prime minister had described the southern desert as "Israel's greatest hope for the future," and declared that "Just as the Negev contains hidden resources, so does man; but it is in the Negev that man can become conscious of his hidden powers, arousing him to tap them and put them to creative use."

Ben-Gurion's passionate attachment to the desert was rooted in practical concern: With an area of 5,400 square miles, the Negev made up about 65 percent of the new nation, forming a natural buffer zone for defense and a vital link to the Red Sea and the countries beyond the Indian Ocean. Here, he believed, was the vital living space for Israel's future immigrant population and for its anticipated factories and towns.

Yet at the inception of Israel's statehood, the Negev was largely terra incognita — a weird desolation of sand and scrub, bare rock striated with lurid colors, chasms, canyons and strange craters, mountains carved into fantastic shapes. The heat sits on the land like a weight, and sometimes a blistering east wind — the khamsin — blows for days on end, dry as a furnace, making any activity, even sleep, difficult. Buried under the sands of the desert are the ruined cities of the Nabateans and Byzantines, who succeeded in cultivating parts of the Negev during the first millennium A.D.

But in 1948, the only town in the Negev was Beersheba, with 3,000 inhabitants; it was a market place for the 15,000 Bedouin grazing their flocks in the region and a rough-and-ready frontier post for the farmers of 27 Jewish villages, whose fields were supplied with water from 125 miles of fire hoses that had last seen service in the London Blitz. There were no proper roads; when Israeli forces mounted an attack on the Egyptian army during the War of Independence, they had to hastily excavate a sand-covered Roman road known only to a few archeologists, including Yigael Yadin, who was then

During the pecan harvest in Galilee, a toddler looks on as brightly dressed Arab women gather nuts for a cooperative Jewish farming settlement. Arabs fill approximately 50 percent of the agricultural jobs in Israel.

1

chief of operations of the Israeli Defense Forces. And, apart from the presence of potash, there were no known natural resources.

However, Ben-Gurion's belief in the Negev has been vindicated. By the mid-1980s, the population of the area had soared to about 230,000, including approximately 40,000 Bedouin, most of whom had abandoned their nomadic way of life. Some 100,000 people live in Beersheba, the hub of development in the Negev. Roads radiate from it like spokes, linking a necklace of new towns to the north, cutting south across the desert to Eilat, running east to the Dead Sea and west to the new port of Ashdon. Around Beersheba, a green carpet, ragged and incomplete in parts, unrolls over the desert — more than 140,000 acres of irrigated farmland that supports 55,000 people and produces all the vegetables, dairy products and fruit consumed in the Negev.

But not even the National Water Carrier can make the entire desert bloom. And although Israel uses more than 90 percent of all its available water resources, that is sufficient to irrigate only 41 percent of the country's potential farmland, which is why plans are under way to turn sea water from the Mediterranean into fresh water. In the meantime, the bulk of the Negev's wealth comes from minerals — copper ore from Timna, near Eilat; kaolite from Maktesh Ramon, a giant crater in the middle of the desert; and methane gas from the Zohar fields in the northern Negev.

The real mineral treasure chest, though, lying northeast of the Negev, is the Dead Sea, a 47-mile-long turquoise ribbon nestling 1,306 feet below sea level between the biscuit-colored mountains of Jordan and the abrupt, precipi-

tous eastern edge of Judaea. Here all the water of the Jordan that has not been diverted into the National Water Carrier reaches journey's end, to be evaporated by temperatures that often reach 104° F. between May and August. Despite the forbidding name, there is life in this eerily beautiful place: Date palms, vegetables and grains are grown at the oasis of En Gedi, next to a nature reserve that is the last stronghold of a small population of leopards and a thriving herd of Nubian ibex. Tourist buses ply the western shore, ferrying passengers in air-conditioned comfort to Masada, the imposing clifftop fortress where 960 Jewish zealots killed themselves instead of submitting to Roman slavery, and to Qumran, the place where, in 1947, a young Bedouin stumbled on the ancient Judaic documents known as the Dead Sea Scrolls.

The sea is utterly lifeless, for the slow accumulation of minerals carried into it by the Jordan and the wadis of Judaea have made its water 10 times saltier than the Mediterranean; it is so salty that even a nonswimmer with suicidal intentions will float effortlessly on its surface. The mineral content of the sea is staggering: 24.5 trillion tons of magnesium chloride, 13 trillion tons of sodium chloride, seven trillion tons of calcium chloride, one trillion tons of magnesium bromide, plus large quantities of sulfates, cesium, cobalt, lithium, rubidium and manganese.

Tourists pay high prices to stay in resort hotels where they can immerse themselves in this chemical soup or coat themselves with sulfurous Dead Sea mud. Medical evidence seems to support claims that the effects are beneficial. But the serious business of exploiting the Dead Sea's resources takes place at its southern end, at the

Dead Sea Works, close to the spot where God rained fire and brimstone on Sodom and Gomorrah and where Lot's wife was turned into a pillar of salt. The sites where the Cities of the Plain probably stood are now covered by glittering mineral flats, crisscrossed by an intricate system of dikes and evaporation pans.

Prime Minister Ben-Gurion was able to observe the transformation of the desert first hand, having left office in 1953 and joined an agricultural settlement that he had helped found at Sede Boker, 32 miles south of Beersheba. Fourteen months later, he resumed political office, first as minister of defense and then again as prime minister. But in 1963, at the age of 77, he returned to Sede Boker and remained there until his death, in 1973.

Sede Boker is a typical example of the most distinctive, most venerated and most adventurous of Israeli institutions: the kibbutz, an agricultural settlement in which all property is owned in common and all decisions are made collectively. The first kibbutz was established in 1909 by early Zionist immigrants to Palestine at Degania, on the Sea of Galilee. Today, there are about 270 kibbutzim, each embodying the simple principle expounded by 19th-century philosopher Karl Marx: From each according to his abilities, to each according to his needs. The kibbutzim's structure is based on equality in everything: work, housing, food, clothing and child care.

In the early days, the kibbutzim were spartan outposts of Jewish settlement, and their place in the annals of the country was earned by land reclamation, swamp drainage, malaria eradication and guarding of the country's borders. Income came from agriculture, and the land was worked only by their members. Today, however, a typical kibbutz is virtually a garden suburb with spacious lawns, air-conditioned houses, a swimming pool, library, a gym and often even a beauty salon.

Agriculture is still a major occupation; in the mid-1980s, the 100,000 or so kibbutzniks cultivated 42 percent of the available land and produced 50 percent of all its agricultural output. But most of the revenue comes from kibbutz industries, workshops and guest houses, and much of the farm work is now done by hired hands, often Arabs from the nearby villages, or foreign volunteers on short-term visits.

To be a member of a kibbutz is to belong to an élite: Kibbutzniks not only enjoy the best living conditions in the country but can look forward to obtaining the best jobs. And although they make up barely 3 percent of the population, they exert an influence that is way out of proportion to their numbers. The kibbutzim movement has counted among its members three of Israel's first six prime ministers; between 1949 and 1967, about a third of all Cabinet ministers were kibbutz members; and in the Six Day War, 30 percent of the country's air force pilots and 22 percent of the army officers were products of the kibbutz system. Privilege has its price, however; of the

778 fatalities sustained by Israel in the Six Day War, 200 were from kibbutzim.

In theory, membership in a kibbutz is open to any Israeli, but there is no rush to join the ranks. Even at the beginning of the kibbutz movement, 40 years before the establishment of the Jewish state, many settlers found the socialist principles too rigorous and the communal existence too stifling. In 1921, some of them broke away to form a moshav, the prototype for another Israeli experiment in collective living.

A moshav is a cooperative agricultural settlement in which each farmer owns his own home and works his own plot of land, receiving any profit it may yield. All produce is marketed through

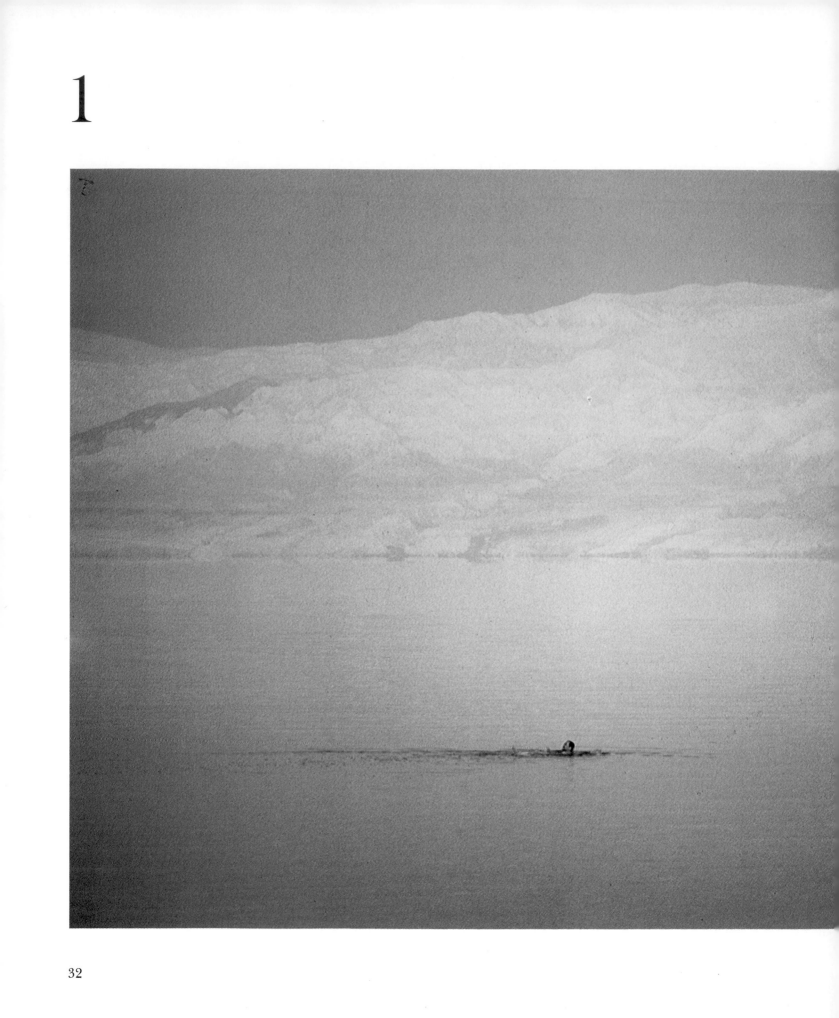

the cooperative, which also helps its members to buy seed, fertilizer and fodder and to obtain credit. It maintains machinery and vehicles, workshops and stores, and it erects and maintains public installations, such as irrigation plants, dairies, schools and clinics. After independence, attempts were made to settle immigrants from widely different backgrounds — such as Rumanian and Moroccan Jews — in a single moshav. But community resistance proved so strong that the policy now is to allow only a single ethnic group, or a number of similar ones, on any one settlement. At the beginning of the 1980s, there were about 350 moshavim with a population of some 130,000.

While the concept of the moshav has been imitated in Africa, Asia and some Latin American countries, the kibbutz has caught the imagination of the world without stimulating the world to emulate it. Even among kibbutz members of the third or fourth generation, there are worries that the movement is anachronistic, restrictive and ideologically compromised.

Outsiders often imagine that the typical Israeli is a kibbutznik, but 85 percent of the population lives in cities and towns. While Israel is best known for its military exploits and pioneering agriculture — significantly, pursuits often closed to Jews of the Diaspora — the development of its urban centers is equally impressive.

Consider Tel Aviv, Israel's largest city. When Ben-Gurion landed in Palestine, Tel Aviv did not exist; the site where it now stands was a bleak expanse of sand dunes north of Jaffa, one of the world's oldest ports: Jonah was said to have sailed from here to meet his destiny with the whale, and it was at Jaffa that the Lebanese cedar wood for King Solomon's Temple in Jerusalem was unloaded.

Tel Aviv's early history is less romantic. It was founded in 1901 by two societies set up by Jaffa Jews, who chose the location for a suburb simply because property there was offered at a reasonable price. Nobody imagined that it would grow into a city; for one thing, the climate is unpleasant: It is oppressively humid in summer, and wet and windy in winter. The impetus for Tel Aviv's rapid growth was provided by the wave of immigration that followed World War I.

In 1921, when its population was about 13,000, Tel Aviv was granted municipal status — the first all-Jewish city in modern history. By 1925, the population had risen to 34,000, and Tel Aviv boasted the first Jewish theaters and the first Jewish secondary school. Its population had risen to 120,000 by 1935, making it the largest urban center in Palestine. In 1936, the port of Jaffa was closed down and a new port was built at Tel Aviv. In 1950, Jaffa was combined with its former suburb to become Tel Aviv – Yafo, the Hebrew version of its old Arab name, Yafa. The ugly duckling had taken over the nest.

Independence and the establishment of Jerusalem as the nation's capital did not halt Tel Aviv's growth. Although the seat of government was transferred, many of the government offices remained in Tel Aviv, along with the headquarters of the main political parties and the offices of all the national newspapers except the *Jerusalem Post*. By the mid-1980s, more than 1,555,000 people — almost one third of Israel's population — lived in the metropolitan area of Tel Aviv. And every day, nearly half of Tel Aviv's workers commuted from outside the city, helping to jam the city streets during the rush hour with about half of all the vehicles in the entire country.

As well as being Israel's commercial heart, Tel Aviv is the country's cultural and social center. Two of Israel's seven universities—an extraordinary number for a country with a population barely more than half that of London or New York City—are in Tel Aviv. About three quarters of Israel's 100 or so publishing houses are based in the city, and they produce about 2,000 titles a year, giving Israel the second-highest per capita book production in the world (Switzerland is the highest). Tel Aviv also boasts dozens of art galleries, six theatrical companies and three concert halls, including the Mann Auditorium, home of the internationally renowned Israel Philharmonic Orchestra, which has a subscription list of 36,000 patrons—more supporters, per capita, than any other orchestra in the world. For informal entertainment, there are innumerable cafés and, of course, the beach.

Most people would agree that Tel Aviv is not a beautiful city. Apart from the inevitable multistory hotel and office buildings and a few outposts of individuality, such as the Eastern European-inspired houses in the "old" center, the conurbation is an ungainly sprawl of four- or five-story prefabricated concrete apartment complexes. The uniformity and lack of inspiration evident in most of Israel's modern urban architecture, however, is the price the nation has had to pay for its tremendous growth and rapid entry into the 20th century.

The ruthless standardization of housing was forced on the government as the only means of providing homes

for the immigrants who flooded into Israel after independence. In 1949, there were more than 100,000 Israelis living under canvas in temporary camps, and thousands more Israelis were arriving every week. Yet within a decade, the camps had been cleared, and between 1948 and 1970, nearly 700,000 homes had been completed, making Israel's rate of housing starts the highest recorded for any nation in proportion to its population. At the time of construction, these houses were modern and well-equipped by the standards of the region: The majority were equipped with baths and inside toilets. But the speed and cheapness of their construction meant that the quality was frequently shoddy, and many housing developments less than 30 years old have subsequently been condemned as slums and demolished.

Since the 1960s, however, the quality

of government-financed housing has improved. Successful attempts have also been made to divert new immigrants away from the main urban centers to new towns that, though still resolutely medium-rise, have won praise for their imaginative planning and attractive landscaping. Typical of these modern developments is Ashdod, a town of about 60,000 people about 25 miles down the coast from Tel Aviv. Ashdod was built from scratch in 1959 as a deepwater port. And by 1966, Ashdod had made Tel Aviv's own facilities redundant, only 30 years after that city had itself usurped Jaffa's position as chief port of the region. The pace of development and change in Israel is bewilderingly swift.

In the development towns as well as in the large cities, most Israelis live in housing that is cooperatively owned and managed by the residents. The system is characteristically Israeli, nurturing a degree of neighborliness that is rare in other countries. Even more close-knit are the *shikunim* — planned developments built for people who already know one another, and who are usually members of the same ethnic groups or professions, or even belong to the same political parties. Thus there are *shikunim* for Polish Jews, journalists and Zionist veterans.

There are *shikunim* on the outskirts of Jerusalem, where the architecture of utility has combined with the politics of expediency to transform the setting of one of the most ancient cities on earth. For 4,000 years, Jerusalem stood alone in a natural theater of hills commanding views across the Judaean wilderness, where prophets communed with God, and beyond to the Hills of Moab across the Dead Sea, where Moses first gazed on the Promised Land. This outlook hardly changed until 1948, when the Israelis erected a modern capital — buildings to house public agencies, ministries and parliament — to the west of the Old City. Since 1967, when the Old City was annexed by Israel, its horizons to the north and west have been obscured by apartment houses hastily built for the influx of Jews. The population, which was only 260,000 at the time of independence, has now risen to more than 750,000.

Nevertheless, Jerusalem remains visually bewitching. Partly it is an effect of the topography, broken by many open spaces, which lends interest to even the most mundane of modern developments. Partly it is an effect of the local stone, which is still used for the façades of most buildings — a creamy pink limestone that seems to have its own luminescence in the clear, high air.

And then there is the Old City, standing on the ruins of its own past and separated from the present by a 400-year-old Turkish wall that encloses 1.5 square miles of vaulted alleys, synagogues, mosques, churches, monasteries and convents.

Jerusalem has few of the assets that usually determine the growth of a great city. It is perched on the crest of the Judaean hills at an altitude varying between 2,000 and 2,600 feet, and its setting not only makes it cold in winter but has made it almost inaccessible for most of its history. It has no agricultural hinterland, no traditional industries, not even an adequate water supply. Its single great resource — and its outstanding asset — is its holiness, which is based on a simple and universal belief: One God.

The whole of the Old City of Jerusalem is a monument to monotheism, but the bloody history of these few acres and the division of the city into Muslim, Armenian, Christian and Jewish quarters is evidence that the more simple and more universal the idea, the more controversial it may prove to be. The pioneering Zionists saw this when they drew up a blueprint for a society in which religion would have very little part.

Even in 1967, the annexation of East Jerusalem was defended on patriotic as well as religious grounds. East Jerusalem's remnant of the ancient Temple's Western Wall was, for most Israelis, a symbol of national regeneration rather than a religious shrine. When they touched it for the first time, they touched the keystone of 4,000 years of history, a tangible link with the origins of a people who had nothing but their collective memory to sustain them during the centuries of wandering. □

His prayers finished, a young worshipper strides purposefully away from the Western Wall. A stop at Judaism's holiest shrine fits as easily into his day as his white prayer shawl tucks under his street clothes.

Hardy goats forage on the desert hillsides of the Negev, as they have done since Abraham's time, some 4,000 years ago.

36

THE LANDSCAPES OF THE BIBLE

The Bible has, for centuries, been the core of Judeo-Christian thought, giving the names and places of the Holy Land symbolic significance the world over. The legends of the patriarchs, the searing words of the prophets and the chronicles of the gospel writers have made such names as Jordan and Jerusalem, Galilee and Jericho, Nazareth and Bethlehem universally familiar, yet dissociated from the reality of any specific mountains, rivers, deserts or towns.

In Israel, such names belong to real places. Archeology and scholarship have amplified the accounts of the Old and New Testaments, so that everywhere in this ancient country the present recalls the past. In the second millennium B.C., the spring-watered hills of Israel saw the nomadic beginnings of the Israelite nation; through its desert wastes the Chosen People fled from captivity in Egypt; and on its broad plains they fought a succession of invaders in defense of the land promised by God. In its austere wilderness, Jesus fasted, and in its waters he baptized his followers.

Such is the heritage of modern Israel—a state that came into existence less than a half century ago, yet a place where every landscape holds echoes of an ancient past.

Now the Lord had said unto Abram,
Get thee out of thy country,
and from thy kindred, and from thy father's house,
unto a land that I will shew thee:

And I will make of thee a great nation,
and I will bless thee and make thy name great;
and thou shalt be a blessing:

And Abram was very rich in cattle, in silver,
and in gold.

Genesis 12:1,2; Genesis 13:2

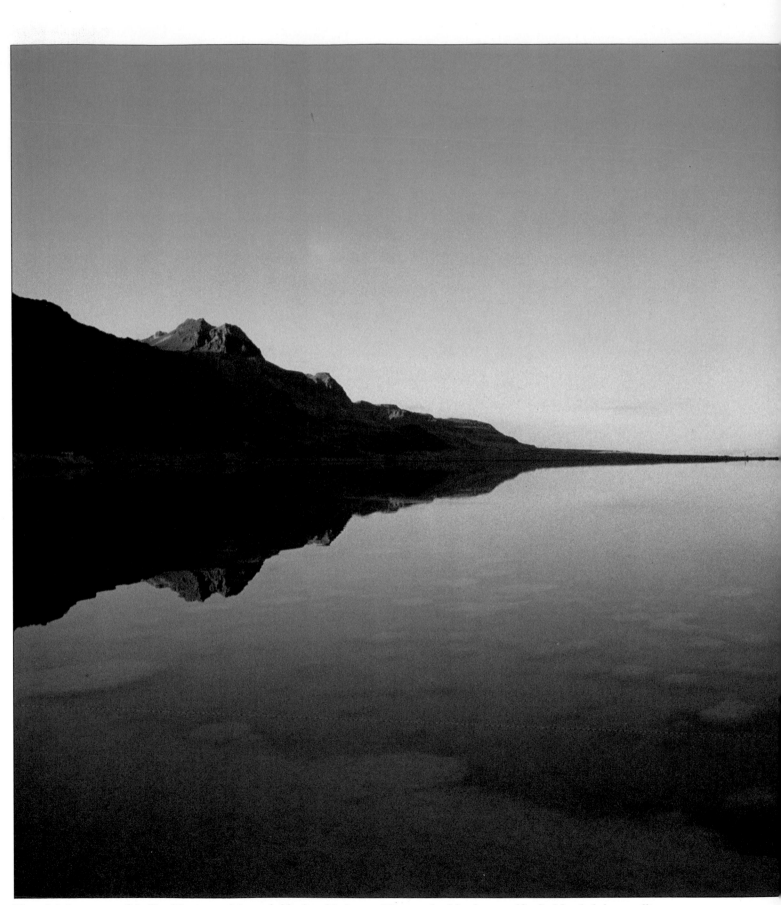

The salt-laden waters of the Dead Sea conceal the probable site of Sodom and Gomorrah, cities destroyed by God for their immorality.

Overlooking the Dead Sea is a pillar-like salt formation, one of several known as Lot's Wife.

The sun was risen upon the earth
when Lot entered into Zoar.

Then the Lord rained upon Sodom and Gomorrah,
brimstone and fire from the Lord out of heaven;

And he overthrew those cities, and all the plain,
and all the inhabitants of the cities,
and that which grew upon the ground.

But his wife looked back from behind him
and she became a pillar of salt.

Genesis 19:23-26

And the Lord said unto him,
This is the land which I sware
    unto Abraham,
unto Isaac, and unto Jacob, saying,
I will give it unto thy seed:
I have caused thee to see it
    with thine eyes,
but thou shalt not go over thither.

So Moses the servant of the Lord
    died there in the land of Moab,
according to the word of the Lord.

Deuteronomy 34:4-5

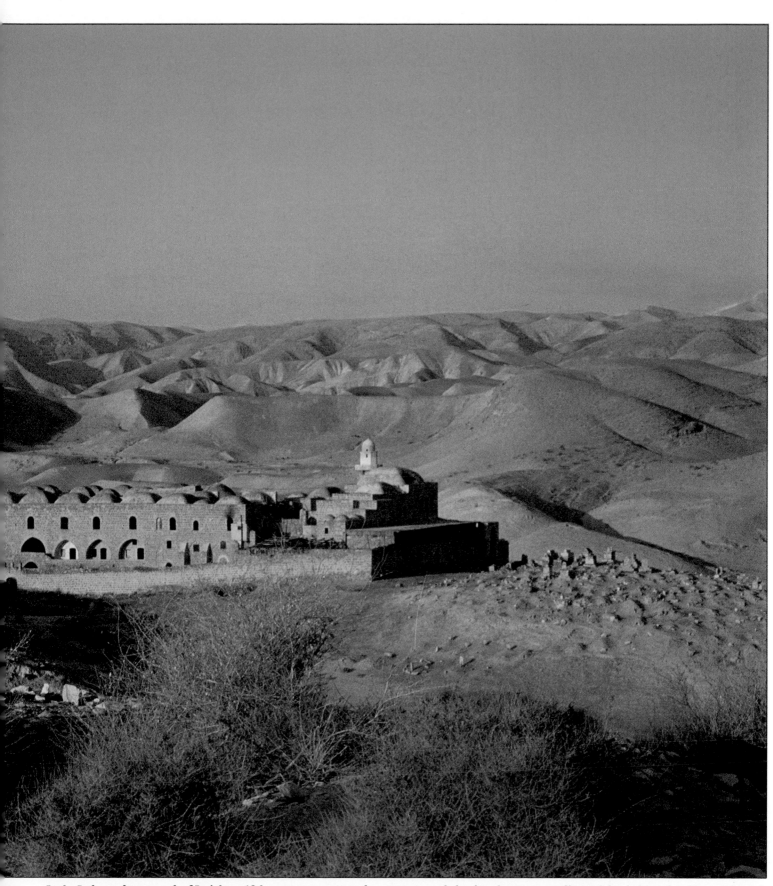

In the Judaean desert south of Jericho, a 13th-century mosque and a cemetery mark the site where — according to Islamic legend — Moses is buried.

And it came to pass in those days,
that Jesus came from Nazareth of Galilee,
and was baptized of John in Jordan.

And straightaway coming up
*   out of the water,*
he saw the heavens opened,
and the Spirit like a dove
*   descending upon him.*

Mark 1:9-10

The green-fringed River Jordan, in the fertile north of Israel, flows for 225 miles before emptying into the Dead Sea.

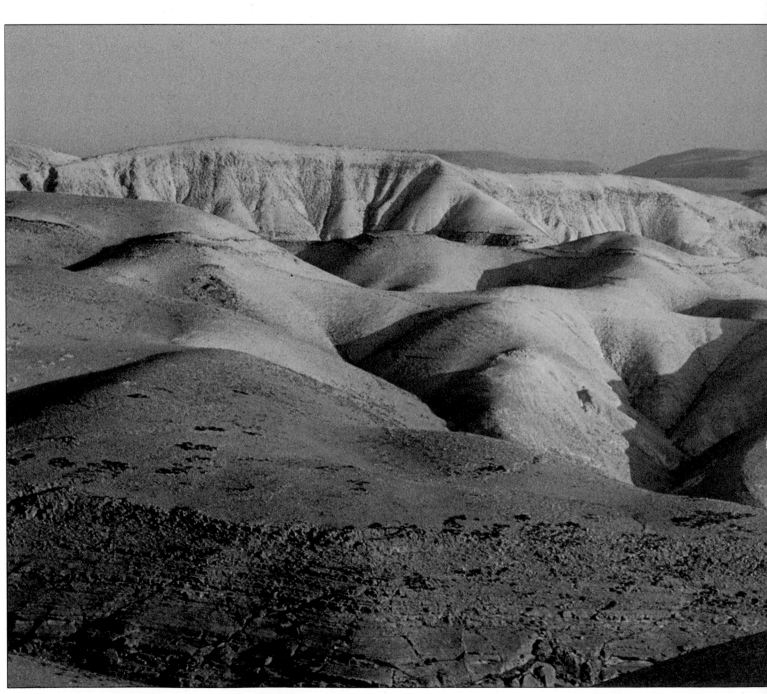

Only a few miles from Jerusalem, the barren hills of the Judaean wilderness offered a retreat for those who, like John the Baptist and Jesus, wished to

44

Then was Jesus led up of the spirit into the wilderness
  to be tempted of the devil.

And when he had fasted forty days and nights,
he was afterward an hungred.

And when the tempter came to him, he said,
If thou be the Son of God,
command that these stones be made bread.

Matthew 4:1-3

devote themselves to fasting and meditation.

Two men fish the choppy waters of the Sea of Galilee, where Jesus found his first disciples — Simon (later called Peter), Andrew, James and John.

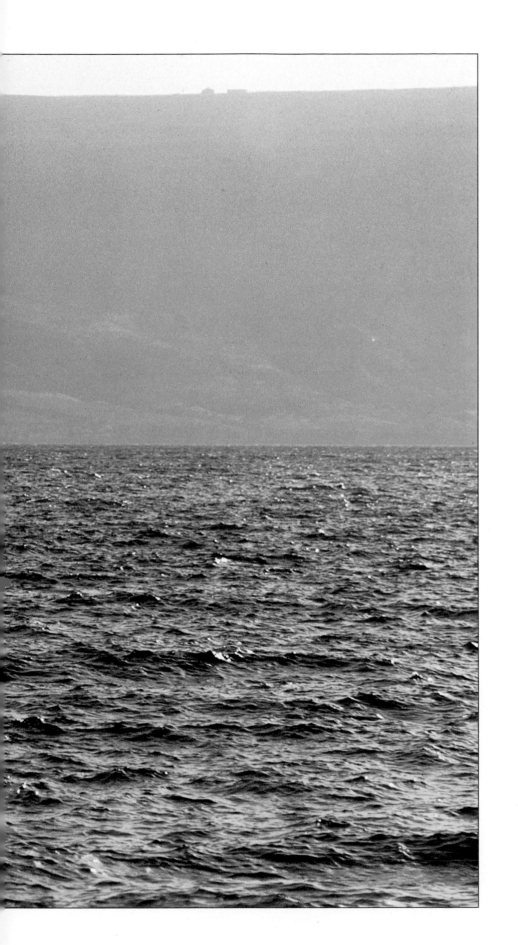

*Now as he walked by the sea of Galilee,
he saw Simon and Andrew his brother
    casting a net into the sea:
for they were fishers.*

*And Jesus said unto them,
Come ye after me, and I will make you
    to become fishers of men.*

Mark 1:16-17

From the gentle slope of the Mount of Olives — now dominated by the spires of a Russian Orthodox church — Jesus rode in triumph into Jerusalem.

And they came to a place which was named Gethsemane:
and he saith to his disciples,
Sit ye here, while I shall pray.

And he went forward a little, and fell on the ground,
and prayed that if it were possible,
the hour might pass from him.

Mark 14:32,35

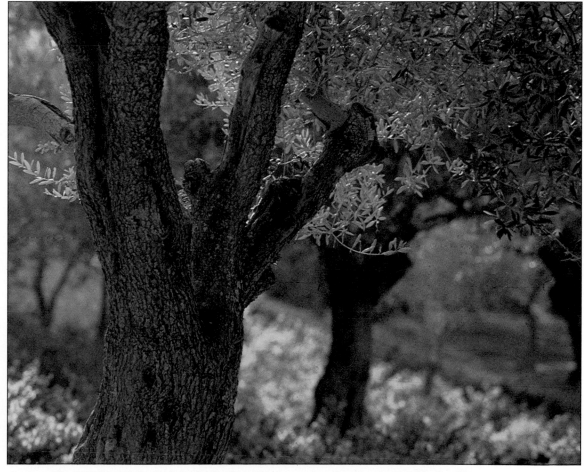

Ancient olive trees cast their shade in the Garden of Gethsemane, where Jesus prayed before his arrest.

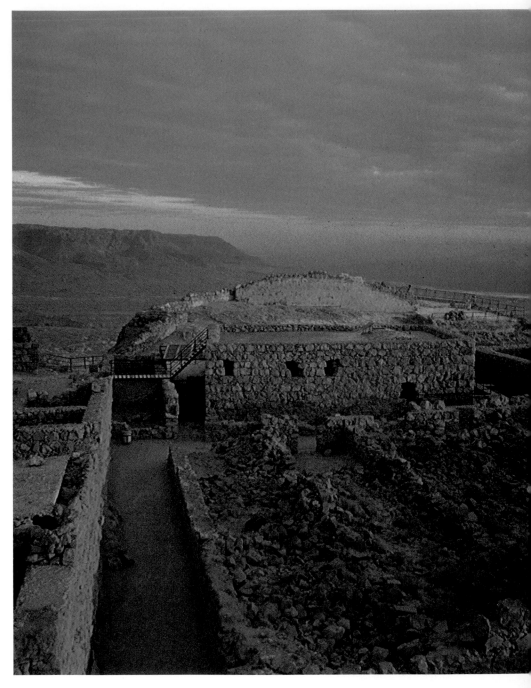

CENTURIES OF EXILE AND RETURN

On a rock above the Dead Sea, the fortress of Masada stands as a potent symbol of the struggle against tyranny. It was here, in 73 A.D., that 960 Jewish resistance fighters — men, women and children — chose to commit mass suicide rather than surrender to the besieging Romans.

Throughout their long, stateless centuries, the Jews never lost their yearning for the Promised Land. Three times a day during prayers the pious would repeat the words: "Sound the great horn for our freedom, lift up the banner to gather our exiles and gather us from the four corners of the earth to our land." They were not advocating a practical policy: The Return was scheduled for "the end of days" and would take place under the divine authority of the Messiah, come at last to deliver the Chosen People. The duty of the Jews, in the interminable meantime, was to keep the faith; in short, to remember.

No people, perhaps, has more to remember than the Jews. Their recorded history is longer than that of any other race. The exile that began almost 2,000 years ago and ended with the birth of modern Israel in 1948 is merely one episode in their saga.

In the second millennium B.C., the patriarch Abraham, commanded by God to found a nation of people who would serve a single deity, set off with his flocks and his kin from the ancient city of Ur, near the Arabian Gulf, to the land of Canaan, lying roughly between the Jordan River, the Dead Sea and the Mediterranean. "Unto thy seed," said the One God to Abraham, in Genesis, "will I give this land." Such was the promise that inspired Abraham's heirs, the Israelites.

Here history blends inextricably with legend: Abraham may not have existed and the Biblical account, which was written well after the supposed journey to Canaan, is more spiritual than historical. Nevertheless, archeological evidence does not contradict it. Abraham, or a number of Abrahams, probably did make such a journey. The important part of the legend is that before the Jews were a people they were an idea; the monotheism of Abraham was a long way from fully developed Judaism, but it was even more distant from the polytheistic cults of the patriarch's neighbors.

The next great step was the first exile. Driven by famine from Canaan, the Israelites moved to Egypt, where their status gradually changed from that of welcomed immigrants to a persecuted and enslaved minority. Around 1200 B.C., under the leadership of Moses (again possibly a legendary figure, though the archeological record supports the outline of the story), they fled from their oppressors and journeyed across the Sinai peninsula until they came to Mount Sinai. At the summit, God gave Moses the Ten Commandments, which were to serve as the basis of both Judaic law (the Torah) and Christianity. Moses also received a renewed injunction to lead his people back into the land of Canaan and there to create "a holy nation."

Thenceforth, the story of the Jews moves steadily out of legend and into history. For two centuries, their nation developed without a central authority;

2

In a medieval Haggadah — the ritual text for the Passover feast — the Egyptian Pharaoh consults his wise men, and a blue-robed Moses leads escaping Israelites through the Red Sea. The annual Passover festival commemorates the flight from slavery in Egypt.

in the Bible this was the time of the Judges — divinely inspired individuals who were sometimes military heroes and sometimes judicial officials. The people were mostly small farmers, owing allegiance more to one of the 12 tribes into which they were divided than to the community as a whole.

But the threat from warlike neighbors, especially the Philistines, brought the 12 tribes together under a joint monarchy, and Israel entered the age of Kings: Saul, David and Solomon being the earliest. The capital was Jerusalem; there, in the 10th century B.C., Solomon built the First Temple to house the Tablets of the Law that Moses had received on Mount Sinai.

After Solomon's death, the old tribal feuds flared up again, and the nation split into two kingdoms — Israel, with its new capital of Samaria, in the north, and Judah, centered on Jerusalem, in the south. The division proved disastrous in the face of the rising empire of Assyria. In 721 B.C., the Assyrians descended from the northeast upon Samaria, laid it waste and carried off thousands of Israelites — the fabled Ten Lost Tribes — into slavery.

Judah fared better. Although it was forced to accept Assyrian suzerainty, it continued to exercise almost complete autonomy. Nevertheless, the country remained easy prey for avaricious powers. Over the next six centuries, Judah was ruled, in turn, by Babylonians, Persians and Greeks.

The Jews retained a fierce national pride, however, and in 114 B.C., after almost 50 years of guerrilla warfare against their Greek masters, they finally succeeded in reestablishing an independent Judah.

Independence did not last for long. In 63 B.C., the country was overrun by

An illumination from a 1470 Jewish prayer book depicts Haman, would-be slayer of the Persian Jews, executed with his sons. Foiled by Queen Esther, the king's Jewish wife, Haman was hanged and the Jews were saved — an event marked by the festival of Purim.

yet another set of conquerors: the Romans. At first, the Romans did little more than change the name of their new domain from Judah to Judaea. Over the years, however, their rule became increasingly oppressive. In 66 A.D., led by a group of militant patriots known as Zealots, the Jewish population rose in open revolt. The Roman garrison of Jerusalem was massacred, and a Roman army that was sent to salvage the situation was cut to pieces.

For a while, the Jewish rebels were helped by a bitter civil war that had broken out within the empire. But in 70 A.D., a powerful Roman army captured Jerusalem and the city was razed.

Jerusalem's fall marked the end of the so-called Great Revolt. The surviving Zealots fled to the fortress of Masada, on a grim, granite rock above the Dead Sea. Here, they held out for another three years; even at the end, in the face of overwhelming odds, they refused to surrender. Instead, the Zealots killed first their wives and children, then themselves.

The spirit of resistance did not die at Masada. Less than 60 years later, Simon Bar-Kochba — "Son of a Star" — led a new uprising that drove the Romans out of the country. They soon returned, however, and by 135 A.D. Jewish independence had been utterly crushed. A Jewish state would not be seen again for another 1,813 years.

The damage done by the Great Revolt had been bad enough; the consequences of the Bar-Kochba rebellion were far worse. Whatever Jewish buildings had survived in Jerusalem were demolished and plowed under, and by imperial decree all Jews were barred, on pain of death, from coming within sight of their ancient city, which was to be reconstructed as a Roman colony and renamed Aeolia Capitolina. The country itself was a waste, with many of its inhabitants dead or sold into slavery. Even the name Judaea was obliterated from the maps. The land was to be called Syria Palaestina, after the most detested of the Jews' ancient enemies, the Philistines.

When the danger to Roman rule had passed, however, the empire was satisfied, and it was not long before the synagogues and rabbinical academies of Palestine were flourishing once more. But the Jewish population had been decimated by war. Palestine remained the spiritual center of the Jewish world, but its political and economic center lay outside the homeland, among the Jews of the Diaspora.

The Diaspora, or Disperal, was no new phenomenon. Jews had been leaving the homeland for centuries, and deportation by conquering armies was only one of the causes. Venturesome Jews had long sought their fortunes abroad, and their communities were scattered throughout the empire.

The oldest part of the Diaspora, in fact, was outside the empire altogether, in Mesopotamia, once the homeland of Babylonians. In 586 B.C., the Babylonians had destroyed Jerusalem and taken its people into captivity, and a Babylonian Jewish community had existed ever since. The Babylonian Jews produced, by the end of the fifth century, one of the greatest of all Jewish achievements — the Talmud, or Teaching, a judicial, theological and practical guide that even today orders every aspect of observant Jewish life.

By the time the Talmud was completed, the situation of the Jews within the Roman Empire had deteriorated sharply. The catalyst for their misfortunes was an edict proclaimed by the Emperor Constantine in 313 A.D., which made Christianity effectively the state religion. To evangelistic Christians, the Jews were anathema. Not only did they bear a blood-guilt for the Crucifixion of Jesus, but they persisted in denying Christ's divinity, claiming that the true Messiah had yet to appear. It followed, therefore, that they were not merely misguided, but were an unclean and pernicious sect deserving any form of persecution that Christians saw fit to inflict on them.

Within a few years of Constantine's edict, a mass of discriminatory laws were passed, stripping Jews of land and civil rights, and forcing them out of the mainstream of the economy. Soon synagogue-burning became rife, and at the beginning of the fifth century, in Alexandria, Jews suffered their first full-scale massacre.

In Palestine itself, which the Roman Empire now regarded as not merely a province but as the Holy Land, the Jews were a small and persecuted minority, eking out a living in the most desolate corners of the country and entirely at the mercy of the assortment of illiterate, bigoted monks, fanatical Christian pilgrims and Christian brigands who now largely inhabited it.

The other great world-conquering religion of the first millennium was kinder to the Jews. The new monotheistic creed of Islam arose in Arabia in the seventh century. The faith spread with extraordinary speed, and by the eighth century, its followers had created an Islamic empire that stretched all the way from the borders of India to the Atlantic Ocean. Palestine itself was conquered in 638 A.D.

The empire's Arab rulers, who wanted to make the most of the loyal service

Holding a whip to symbolize his authority, the first-century Jewish sage, Rabban Gamaliel the Elder, addresses students. According to Saint Paul's account in the New Testament, it was "at the feet of Gamaliel" that Paul received his religious education.

that Jews were willing to offer, not only allowed them to practice their religion without interference, but also freed them from the economic and cultural restrictions that had been imposed on them under Christianity. As a result, Jews reached high positions in every sphere of life, from trade to diplomacy. In Palestine, Jews were permitted to settle once more in Jerusalem, while returning exiles were given the right to reclaim their land.

Islam reached Spain in 711 A.D., creating a hospitable environment for the Jews already settled there. For many centuries thereafter, a rich Hispano-Judaic culture flourished. The Hebrew word for Spain was "Sepharad," from which the Spanish Jews took the name of Sephardim. Intellectual life blossomed; Jewish scholarship made the University of Cordoba the greatest center of learning in Europe.

The lessons of coexistence offered by the Islamic lands were not lost on the more perceptive rulers of the Christian West, who saw the advantages that their own Jewish communities could bring them. Not the least of these was the access to the web of trade and communications that Jews had painfully built up both in Christendom and in the Islamic world.

A period of relative calm and stability ensued for European Jewry. It was abruptly shattered in 1096, when France and other Western European countries launched a Crusade to liberate Palestine from the Muslim infidels. Since the intention was to kill nonbelievers, many Christian warriors decided to start with the nearest Jews, so that the route to the Holy Land became littered with Jewish corpses.

And when, in 1099, the Crusaders eventually conquered Jerusalem, they

This sixth-century mosaic, discovered in a ruined Byzantine church at Medaba, near the Dead Sea, is the oldest known map of Jerusalem. More than 30 buildings can be identified on it, including the Damascus Gate *(below, left)* and the Church of the Holy Sepulcher *(center)*.

marked their victory by the murder of every non-Christian in the city. The only surviving Jews were herded into a synagogue and burned alive.

By the time the Muslims recaptured the Holy Land in 1291, anti-Semitism was endemic throughout Western Europe. Jews found themselves subjected to harsh taxation, sometimes forced to wear distinguishing badges, and penned into ghettos — the word was first applied to the Jewish quarter of Venice in 1516, but the reality had long anticipated it.

Far from extinguishing the Jewish sense of identity, persecution strengthened it. Physical segregation, imposed by European authorities to prevent the contamination of Christians by Jews,

was often welcomed by Jewish leaders as a means of preventing the reverse. Judaism depended on the observation of Talmudic Law; separation from Christians ensured that the Jews had no other law to seduce them.

After discrimination and persecution, there came massacres and mass expulsions: from England in 1290, from France in 1394, and finally, after the Christian reconquest, from the Sephardic heartland of Spain in 1492.

After the expulsions, the dividing lines of the Diaspora were even more diverse. The Sephardim traveled north, south and east, joining existing Jewish communities in Holland, North Africa and the Balkans. The German Jews — the name Ashkenazim comes from the Hebrew word for the Germanic lands — moved primarily eastward, into Poland, Lithuania and Russia. The two waves met in the territories of the Islamic Ottoman Empire, ruled by the sultans of Turkey, who offered not only a refuge but a welcome.

In 1517, the Ottomans made themselves masters of Palestine, the homeland to which the Jews still looked back longingly in their prayers and traditions. Palestine was to remain part of the Ottoman Empire for the next four centuries.

Not surprisingly, some of the more pious Jews took the opportunity of returning to Palestine. They went back, though, not as colonists but as pilgrims. According to their belief, the rebirth of the Jewish nation was something that could only be accomplished with the coming of the Messiah and the ingathering of his scattered people.

It was not, indeed, until the end of the 19th century that Jews began to consider seriously the idea of a Jewish nation created ahead of the Messiah's coming. The impetus was the desperation of the Jews in Tsarist Russia. Unlike their brethren in the West, who now enjoyed the fruits of emancipation, the Russian Jews continued to live under conditions hardly different from those their forebears had known in the Middle Ages. Denied all rights of citizenship, they were the helpless victims of both state oppression and mob violence.

Even so, the anti-Jewish frenzy that followed the assassination of Tsar Alexander II in 1881 — as with all great calamities at that time, the Jews were held responsible — took the world by surprise. On a scale that had not been seen for more than a century, murder and arson ravaged the Jewish community and sent hundreds of thousands of terrified refugees streaming across Russia's frontiers. A new word entered the European vocabulary: pogrom.

The mass violence did more than drive Russian Jews westward. It inspired in some of them a desperate conviction that freedom and safety were to be found only within the borders of a Jewish homeland. As Leo Pinsker, a Russian-Jewish physician, wrote in his book *Auto-Emancipation,* published in 1882, "We must reestablish ourselves as a living nation."

Some of Pinsker's young admirers tried to put this idea into practice, forming a back-to-Zion agricultural movement that they called BILU, from the Hebrew initials of a Biblical phrase: "House of Jacob, come let us go!" But Palestine was far away; money was scarce; and friends were few. The first party to make the return comprised precisely 16 people.

It was a very small beginning. It might have been the ending, too, but for the inspiration and energy of one man. Theodor Herzl, who was born in Budapest in 1860, was a journalist by trade. He was also at one time so indifferent a Jew that he felt that the mass baptism of Jewish children might be the answer to anti-Semitism.

Herzl's moment of truth came when he went to Paris to cover the infamous Dreyfus trial in 1894. Captain Alfred Dreyfus, a Jewish officer in the French army, was accused of being a German spy. The evidence of treason was slim, that of anti-Jewish prejudice strong; but what shocked the young Herzl was the crowd outside the courtroom, in supposedly enlightened France, baying "Death to the Jews!"

With the single-minded devotion of an Old Testament prophet, Herzl wrote one of the most influential tracts of all time: *The Jewish State*. He had heard of neither Pinsker nor the BILU movement. He was equally ignorant of the obstacles in his path, from the physical difficulties of colonizing Palestine to the opposition facing him from his fellow Jews, especially the wealthiest and most influential.

Perhaps it was his ignorance that gave him strength, for by 1897, he was able to convene the first Zionist Congress, which was held in Basel, Switzerland. Many Western Jews were horrified, believing that it would only encourage anti-Semitism and undermine the process of Jewish assimilation. Others, however, were less timid and the Congress turned out to be a triumphant success. Afterward, Herzl declared, "At Basel, I created the Jewish State. In five years, perhaps, and certainly in 50, everyone will see it." It was the sort of outrageous statement only a visionary can make. Incredibly, it turned out to be true.

Over the next few years, Herzl was tireless, knocking at every door, seeking help from the governments of France, Britain and Germany, negotiating with the sultan of Turkey, even pleading with the pope. Yet still the great prize remained out of reach, and Herzl, exhausted by his efforts, died at the age of 44 in 1904.

The Zionist movement had little time

A contemporary painting shows the 16th-century Turkish sultan, Suleiman the Magnificent, receiving a foreign ambassador. Although the Holy Land prospered under Suleiman's rule, decline set in with his death, and for the next 350 years, Palestine languished.

to mourn him: There was much to do, not least in Palestine itself. Like the rest of the Ottoman Empire, the country had fallen into chronic decay, with the result that it was now largely barren, exploited by corrupt Turkish officials and ravaged by drought, banditry and disease. The Zionist pioneers remained undaunted, however, and by 1914, they had managed to set up 44 settlements, an agricultural school and a technical college.

Over this scene of gradual progress, World War I burst like a thunderclap. With the great powers locked in conflict, it seemed unlikely that any of them would be paying much attention to the Zionists. Worse still, Turkey and Russia were on different sides — the former had allied itself with Germany and Austria, and the latter with France and Britain. This meant that the majority of Palestinian Jews, being of Russian origin, were regarded by the Turks as enemy aliens, and many were expelled from the country. It was this period of cataclysmic upheaval, however, that was to bring Zionism its greatest triumph to date.

One of the leading Zionists, Chaim Weizmann (by origin a Russian Jew), was a chemist of world stature lecturing at Manchester University. A discovery he had made in explosives manufacture brought him into contact with the highest levels of the British government, and he used every opportunity to advance his people's claim.

By the winter of 1916, the British were prepared to do more than just listen. The war was going badly: Britain was blockaded by German U-boats; Russia was on the brink of revolution and collapse; and the United States was still hesitant to enter the conflict. But if the American and Russian Jews could

c. 7000 B.C. Neolithic settlers build Jericho, the oldest known city, complete with wall, temple and moat.

c. 2000 B.C. Abraham, the Biblical patriarch from whom Jewish people trace their ancestry, travels from Mesopotamia to the Land of Canaan.

c. 1700-1290 B.C. Driven by famine from Canaan into Egypt, the Israelites are gradually reduced to slavery.

c. 1290 B.C. Moses leads the Israelites out of Egypt. During their 40 years of wandering in the deserts of Sinai they receive the Ten Commandments.

c. 1250-1225 B.C. Joshua leads the 12 tribes of Israel back into the Promised Land of Canaan.

c. 1020 B.C. Under Saul, the Israelites establish a monarchy in an effort to resist expansion of the Philistines.

c. 1004 B.C. Saul falls in battle against the Philistines and the kingdom is split between the northern and southern groups of tribes.

c. 998-965 B.C. The kingdom is reunited under David, who crushes the Philistines and sets up his capital at Jerusalem.

c. 965-926 B.C. The crown passes to David's son, Solomon (above), who erects the First Temple in Jerusalem.

c. 926 B.C. With Solomon's death, the country splits once more. The northern kingdom calls itself Israel and the southern kingdom becomes Judah.

733 B.C. Judah submits to the growing might of the Assyrians.

721 B.C. Israel is conquered by the Assyrians, and many of its people — the Ten Lost Tribes — are deported.

597-586 B.C. Nebuchadnezzar II, king of the Babylonians, rules Judah as a vassal state. Twelve years later, in the wake of a Jewish revolt, Nebuchadnezzar destroys the city of Jerusalem, including the First Temple, and forces most of the population into exile in Babylon.

538 B.C. Cyrus, king of the Persians, conquers Babylon and grants Jews permission to return to Jerusalem and rebuild the Temple.

332 B.C. Alexander the Great brings Judah under Macedonian rule.

198 B.C. Judah is conquered by the Seleucid rulers of Syria.

167-114 B.C. A Jewish revolt against the Seleucids is crushed and the warrior-patriot, Judah Maccabee, dies in battle. But a prolonged guerrilla war ends with the reestablishment of Jewish independence.

63 B.C. Judah is occupied by the Romans, who rename it Judaea.

33 A.D. Jesus is crucified (below).

66-74 The Jews, inspired by a militant group known as the Zealots, launch the Great Revolt against Rome. The Romans destroy Jerusalem, including the Second Temple, and the surviving Zealots take refuge at the fortress of Masada. Outnumbered by Romans, they prefer suicide to capture.

132-135 Final revolt of the Jews against Rome is led by Simon Bar-Kochba. After three years, the revolt is crushed. Jews are prohibited from entering Jerusalem and Judaea is renamed Syria Palaestina as a reminder of their ancient foes, the Philistines.

325 Constantine I, the first Christian emperor, begins the transformation of Jerusalem into a Christian city.

638 Palestine is conquered by the Arabs. For the next 460 years, the country remains under Muslim rule.

691 Caliph Abd al-Malik completes the building of the Dome of the Rock, one of Islam's holiest shrines.

1096 Prompted by an appeal issued by Pope Urban II, soldiers from France and other Christian lands launch a Crusade to free Palestine from Muslim rule.

1099-1291 Having conquered Jerusalem, the Crusaders try to turn Palestine into a Christian kingdom. But their rule is threatened by continual rebellion and invasion. In 1187, Jerusalem itself is captured by the Kurdish leader, Saladin, and 104 years later, the last Crusader stronghold of Acre falls to the Mameluke Turks, now undisputed masters of the Holy Land.

1517 The Mamelukes are defeated by Turkish Sultan Selim I. For the next four centuries Palestine remains a province of the Ottoman Empire.

1882 Large-scale violence against Russian Jews prompts the publication of Leo Pinsker's *Auto-Emancipation,* urging the creation of a Jewish national home. Several thousand Jews from Europe travel to Palestine to set up agricultural communities (above).

1896-1897 Theodor Herzl publishes *The Jewish State,* calling for the creation of a Jewish state by international agreement. Herzl organizes the first Zionist Congress at Basel, Switzerland.

1914 In World War I, the Ottoman Empire sides with Germany and Austria against France, Britain and Russia.

1917 British Foreign Secretary Arthur Balfour declares that his government favors "the establishment in Palestine of a National Home for the Jewish people." A few weeks later, British troops enter Jerusalem.

1920 The League of Nations assigns Britain a mandate to govern Palestine. Jewish immigration is renewed.

1933 The Nazi takeover in Germany leads to a massive increase in Jewish immigration to Palestine.

1936-1939 A campaign of violence by the Palestinian Arabs results in almost 5,000 casualties, including 2,849 killed.

1939-1945 During World War II, most Palestine Jews support the British war effort. But British restrictions on Jewish immigration eventually provoke a campaign of bombing and shooting by Jewish extremist groups.

1947 Britain refers the Palestine problem to the United Nations, which votes to partition the country into Arab and Jewish states. The plan is rejected by the Arabs, who renew their attacks on the Jewish population.

1948 The British withdraw and the State of Israel is proclaimed. A day later, the new state is invaded by the armies of five Arab countries.

1949 Israel signs armistice agreements with its Arab neighbors. Jordan bars Israeli access to holy sites in East Jerusalem. Chaim Weizmann is elected Israel's first president, with David Ben-Gurion as prime minister.

1950 The Knesset — Israel's parliament — passes the Law of Return, confirming the right of every Jew to live in Israel.

1956 Egypt nationalizes the Suez Canal, provoking military action by France and Britain. Israel attacks Egyptian bases in Sinai and succeeds in opening the Gulf of Aqaba (Eilat) to Israeli ships.

1962 Twelve stained glass windows by Marc Chagall, depicting the 12 tribes of Israel, are installed at the Hadassah Medical Center, Jerusalem *(left)*.

1964 Arab leaders set up the Palestine Liberation Organization (PLO).

1967 In the Six Day War, Israel wrests the Golan Heights, Sinai, the Gaza Strip and East Jerusalem from the Arabs. The Knesset later approves annexation of the Golan Heights and East Jerusalem, declaring the reunited city "the capital of Israel for all time."

1968 The PLO steps up its terrorist campaign against Israel.

1969 Golda Meir is installed as Israel's fourth prime minister *(below)*.

1973 Egypt and Syria choose the Jewish Day of Atonement to launch an attack against Israeli positions on the Golan Heights and in Sinai, sparking the Yom Kippur War. Israel retains the Golan Heights, but gives up land in Sinai to Egypt. Israel's first prime minister, David Ben-Gurion, dies.

1977 Egyptian President Anwar Sadat meets with Israeli leaders *(below)*.

1979 Under the terms of a peace treaty signed with Egypt, Israel agrees to pull out its remaining forces in Sinai.

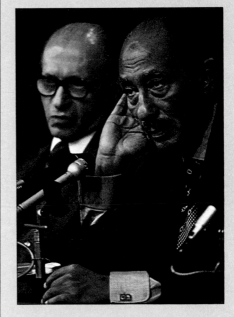

1982-1986 Israel's attempt to drive the PLO out of Lebanon leads to fighting between the Christians and their Druze, Muslim and Palestinian rivals. After the massacre of 800 Palestine civilians by members of a Christian militia force linked to Israel, Israeli Defense Minister Ariel Sharon resigns.

1986 Israel's annual inflation rate — having reached a high of almost 450 percent in 1984 — is reduced to about 22 percent by such measures as a budget cut, a devaluation of the shekel, and wage and price freezes.

2

be persuaded to use their influence on behalf of the Allies, then the situation might be transformed.

Such, at any rate, was the view of the British government. On November 2, 1917, Foreign Secretary Arthur Balfour issued the declaration that afterward bore his name.

The key paragraph read: "His Majesty's Government view with favor the establishment in Palestine of a national home for the Jewish people, and will use their best endeavors to facilitate the achievement of this object, it being clearly understood that nothing shall be done which may prejudice the civil and religious rights of existing non-Jewish communities in Palestine, or the rights and political status enjoyed by Jews in any other country."

It was worded with studied vagueness: It had to be. The British had also been making promises to the Arabs in the Ottoman Empire, with the object of encouraging them (successfully, as it turned out) to revolt against their masters. It was going to be difficult, after the war, to reconcile these pledges.

Nevertheless, the Balfour Declaration represented an astonishing commitment on the part of a great imperial power. And although it was intended primarily to advance British interest, many of the people involved, including Balfour himself, acted out of a genuine sense of idealism. Certainly, it was a triumph for Weizmann's quiet, ceaseless diplomacy — the result, he said later, of 2,000 interviews. (Although he was not elected head of the World Zionist Organization until 1920, he had long been its leading advocate.)

Of course, it was only a beginning: The Balfour Declaration carefully avoided any mention of Jewish statehood. Weizmann himself warned his fellow Zionists that "states must be built up slowly, gradually, systematically and patiently." But now, at least, there was something to build on.

Little more than a month after the

Balfour Declaration, British troops entered the city of Jerusalem. And in September of 1918, a second offensive brought the whole Ottoman Empire down in ruins. The empire capitulated in late October, a few days before the fall of Germany. And Zionists everywhere looked forward optimistically to receiving their due reward.

So, also, did a great many other people. The British, for example, were determined to retain control of the entire area around the Suez Canal, which had become the British Empire's strategic obsession. The French also had imperial ambitions, centered on Syria and Lebanon. And the Arabs, freed at last from the Ottoman yoke, had powerful aspirations of their own.

Between the Arabs and the Zionists, at least, it had seemed that some sort of compromise might be possible. In the closing months of the war, a Zionist commission, headed by Chaim Weizmann, had visited Palestine. Weizmann had met and negotiated with the Emir Feisal, the principal architect of the Arab revolt. The emir, Weizmann later wrote, "was eager to see Jews and Arabs working in harmony," and for the rest of his life, the great Zionist remained convinced that the bitter conflicts that followed in later years could have been avoided.

In 1920, however, the Allies decided on a Middle East settlement that left the Arabs both angry and embittered. France was assigned a League of Nations mandate to govern Syria, and at the same time, Britain received the mandate for Palestine. The Balfour pledge was incorporated in the terms of the Palestine Mandate, and the world Zionist movement was recognized as the appropriate "Jewish Agency" for cooperating with and assisting the British in building a Jewish national home. The high hopes of Arab independence were to a large extent crushed, and from that time on, the Arabs were not in the mood to compromise with anyone.

The Zionists, though, were also in a difficult position. At the end of the war, Jews accounted for barely 10 percent of Palestine's 750,000 inhabitants. And only a small fraction of these Jews were Zionist sympathizers: Most of them lived in pious communities devoted to Talmudic study; they were dependent on Diaspora charity and not supportive of the Zionist notion of a Jewish state. To make the Zionist dream a reality, it was clear that large-scale immigration was essential.

But the British, fearful of Arab reaction, were unwilling to permit it. Zionists had cheered when the British government appointed Sir Herbert (later Lord) Samuel — who was himself a Jew — as the first high commissioner of Palestine. Samuel, however, was first and foremost a representative of the British Crown, and he felt that because he was Jewish, he was obliged to lean toward the Arabs.

Shortly after his arrival, Samuel granted the office of grand mufti of Jerusalem — and with it the religious leadership of Arab Palestine — to Amin al-Husseini, a passionate young nationalist who had fled the country in 1920 to escape imprisonment for inciting anti-Jewish riots. In 1921, the new mufti celebrated his appointment by stirring up fresh riots. To the fury of the Zionists, Samuel responded not by arresting the mufti, but by restricting Jewish immigration.

Samuel, in fact, was taking much the same view as Chaim Weizmann himself: that the national home described in the Balfour Declaration would come about in years rather than months, and that any attempt to hasten the process could only lead to disaster. It was a

In this 1850 lithograph, a party of Polish Jews waits to embark at Jaffa after a pilgrimage to Jerusalem. In the 19th century, many exiles returned to the city of David and Solomon, a focus of aspiration in the Diaspora.

דאָרף אײַך האָבּען! אײַער אלטנײלאַנד

שליסט זיך אָן אין דעם אידישען רעגימענט.

point of view that events in Europe were soon to shatter.

The immediate problem — at least for the Zionists — was not the ban on mass immigration, but the lack of pressure for immigration of any kind. The Russian Jews, who had provided most of the early colonists, were now sealed inside the new Soviet Union, and the Jews who lived in Western Europe and the United States were increasingly reluctant to exchange the comforts and security they enjoyed there for a precarious existence in Palestine. By the late 1920s, the future of the national home looked very shaky indeed. In 1927, there were 2,000 more Jews who left the country than Jews who arrived; and in 1928, the net surplus amounted to 10 people.

It was 1929 that proved to be the most critical year after World War I. The Zionist Congress, at its meeting that August in Zürich, endorsed Weizmann's proposals for an extended Jewish Agency, which would involve the whole of the Diaspora — both the Zionists and the non-Zionists — in the future of Palestine. The decision had more to do with fund raising than power politics, but it aroused fears among the Palestine Arabs that they were at the mercy of just the sort of worldwide Jewish conspiracy that anti-Semites had been ranting about for decades.

Arab fears were inflamed even further by Weizmann's hard-line critic, Vladimir Jabotinsky, who derided any policy that might be construed as appeasement of the Arabs. What Jabotinsky demanded, instead, was an influx of "great colonizing masses" that would establish a Jewish state "on either side of the Jordan." (Although originally part of Palestine, the land immediately to the east of the river had been incorporated into the Emirate of Trans-Jordan, later to become the Hashemite Kingdom of Jordan.)

The result was the worst outbreak of violence so far in the mandate's history. Before British troops could be summoned from Egypt, 133 Jews had died at the hands of Arabs, including 60 members of an ancient, and non-Zionist, religious community. The British authorities put down the rioting, which at times seemed closer to a rebellion, but afterward attempted to apportion blame between the two communities. This naturally infuriated the Jews, who saw themselves, with some justification, as entirely innocent victims. Thus the net effect was not only an increase in Arab-Jewish hostility but a deep-rooted Jewish resentment of the British administration.

The British, in fact, had long held the view that the peaceful implementation of the Balfour Declaration was an impossibility. They reacted characteristically by sending a series of Royal Commissions to study the problem. It was less a policy than a means of marking time. Unfortunately, events unfolding in Europe meant that Britain would have no time to mark.

In January 1933, Adolf Hitler became chancellor of Germany, inaugurating the most appalling persecution in all of Jewish history. The immediate result was a tremendous increase in immigration to Palestine; from 9,533 in 1932, the numbers leaped to the unprecedented level of 61,854 in 1935. The flood of refugees provoked the inevitable Arab response. By 1936, a full-scale rebellion had broken out.

The uprising continued for six months, after which the British appointed yet another Royal Commission. The report of this commission, published in 1937, recommended the end of the mandate and the partition of Palestine into autonomous Jewish and Arab areas. The Jews were inclined to

Jews gather on a sandy wasteland near Jaffa in 1909 to parcel out building lots for the proposed suburb of Tel Aviv — Hill of Spring. Swelled by waves of immigration, Greater Tel Aviv is now Israel's largest city, with a population of more than 1.5 million.

accept the plan, but the British government considered the partition proposals to be unworkable (as, indeed, did the League of Nations itself).

This did not prevent the Arabs, however, from believing that they were to become the victims of Zionist machinations. In the summer of 1937, a second revolt erupted. This time the killing was to continue for two years. Nor were the Palestinian Arabs the only ones to express their outrage at Britain's supposed preferential treatment of the Zionists. A Pan-Arab conference declared: "Britain must change her policy or we shall be at liberty to side with other European powers whose policies are inimical to Great Britain."

By now the war clouds gathering over Europe were obvious even to the appeasement-minded government of Neville Chamberlain, and the threat did not go unheeded. In a war with Germany, the British knew that the Jews would have no alternative but to fight at their side; the Arabs, on the other hand, could easily create serious difficulties, threatening military bases and oil supplies.

For the British government, therefore, the choice was clear. In May 1939, it published a white paper — that is, a declaration of policy — on Palestine that shocked and infuriated Jews. A total of 25,000 Jewish immigrants would be allowed to enter the country immediately; but no more than 10,000 a year would be admitted over the next five years, and thereafter none, unless the Arabs agreed (which seemed unlikely). After 10 years, there was to be established an independent Arab Palestine in which only 5 percent of the land would be alloted for Jewish settlement.

What this white paper amounted to was a virtual repudiation of the Balfour Declaration, and the Jews were understandably bitter. As David Ben-Gurion, the head of the Jewish Agency Executive, stated after the British declaration of war on Germany: "We shall fight with Great Britain in this war as if there were no white paper, and we shall fight the white paper as if there were no war."

More disappointment came when the British refused to allow the Zionists to raise a Jewish army; nevertheless, some 30,000 Palestinian Jews enlisted as individuals in the British forces. Apart from their contribution to the defeat of Nazi Germany, it was becoming clear to Zionist leaders that men

2

with military training were likely to be a vital asset in the years to come.

They already had the Haganah — meaning "Defense" — a clandestine force that had existed in Palestine, with the tacit agreement of the British authorities, since the early 1920s. During the troubled 1930s, the Haganah had provided Jewish settlements with their primary protection against Arab attack; some of its members had even received training from the British. In effect, it was the military arm of the Jewish Agency, and at the outset of World War II, it cooperated with the British to such an extent that it was more or less legally recognized.

As the war progressed, two other small groups of armed Jews began to make their presence felt — and both were entirely illegal. The first was the Irgun (short for Irgun Tsva'i Leumi, or National Military Organization), extremists who had split from the Haganah. The second was the Freedom Fighters of Israel, better known as the Stern Group, itself an offshoot of the Irgun. Increasingly frustrated by British policy, these organizations turned to outright terrorism.

The key issue, as always, was immigration. Ever since 1939, boatloads of desperate Jewish refugees had been reaching Palestine's shores, only to be turned away by British warships. The mandatory policy was to receive immigrants only up to the white paper quota. Any immigrants above the quota were shipped off to detention camps either in Palestine or in some other part of the British Empire. By 1942, when the first inklings of the Nazis' "Final Solution" reached the outside world, British policy began to seem to most Jews to be not merely anti-Zionist but downright murderous.

The growing tension was reflected in a near split in the Zionist movement. Against the patient gradualism of Chaim Weizmann — who was still negotiating for a Jewish army — there arose a younger, angrier faction motivated by a passionate sense of urgency and led by David Ben-Gurion. It had had enough of negotiating. Instead, Ben-Gurion demanded "that the gates of Palestine be opened . . . and that Palestine be established as a Jewish commonwealth, integrated in the structure of the new democratic world."

The extremists of the Irgun and the Stern Group, ignoring opposition from Ben-Gurion and the other mainstream Zionist leaders, set about achieving that Jewish commonwealth with the bullet and the bomb. In a public declaration issued in 1944, the Irgun announced that "there is no longer any armistice between the Jewish people and the British administration that hands our brothers over to Hitler. Our people are at war with this regime, war to the end."

The surrender of Nazi Germany — and, soon afterward, the election in Britain of an avowedly pro-Zionist Labor government — brought only the briefest of respites. In peacetime as well as in war, no British government was willing to accept the wholesale alienation of the Arab world that would result from the entry into Palestine of large numbers of Jewish refugees.

While British ministers, led by Foreign Secretary Ernest Bevin, engaged in a series of fruitless negotiations with Jewish and Arab delegations in London, the situation in Palestine went from bad to worse. Even the Haganah, for so long an example of moderation and restraint, carried out a large number of sabotage attacks that left the country's communications in chaos.

At this juncture, United States President Harry S. Truman infuriated the British leaders by supporting a Jewish Agency demand that 100,000 Jewish refugees be allowed immediate entry to Palestine. However, British Prime Minister Clement Attlee had good reasons for avoiding an open breach with the Americans. In addition to trying to secure a vital loan from the United States for his war-exhausted country, he was also hoping to persuade the Americans to take over some of Britain's responsibilities in Palestine.

Truman proved amenable on the first point but would not be moved on the second, and the most that Attlee was able to achieve was the appointment of an Anglo-American Committee of Inquiry "to examine political, economic and social conditions in Palestine as they bear on the problem of Jewish immigration." The committee published its report in April 1946: The 100,000 immigrants should be admitted — but into a binational state under British protection, where Jew and Arab lived in harmony.

Unfortunately, no such state existed, or was ever likely to exist. Even if it had been a possibility, the British would have had little enthusiasm for protecting it. Too many British servicemen had already died at the hands of the terrorists and the violence was escalating. In June, the Haganah destroyed the Allenby bridge across the Jordan and blew up 13 planes at Lydda airport.

Although both of these operations were conducted without the loss of life, the Palestine administration this time decided to hit back hard by ordering the arrest not only of the Haganah commanders but of the Jewish Agency leaders as well. A few weeks later, the Irgun carried out its own retaliation by

After World War II, British troops board the *Exodus 1947,* an immigrant ship rammed by the Royal Navy and towed into Haifa. Anxious to avoid provoking the Arabs, the ruling British had imposed severe curbs on Jewish entry to Palestine, but many ships tried to land their passengers illegally.

blowing up a wing of the King David Hotel, in Jerusalem, part of which was used as British Army headquarters. British, Jews and Arabs were among the 91 dead and 45 injured.

In his fury, the commanding officer in Palestine issued an order forbidding his men to fraternize with Jews, which would "punish them in a way the race dislikes — through their pockets." Worse still, some of the British troops were starting to take the law into their own hands. A grisly series of atrocities and counteratrocities began.

Politically, the situation remained equally grim. It was not helped by a belligerent Bevin, who declared at the Labor Party Conference of June 1946 that the Americans were pressing for the admission of Jewish refugees to Palestine "because they don't want them in New York." Given the American immigration quotas then in force, there was enough truth in the gibe to hurt, and the Americans never forgave him.

Anglo-American relations were strained still further when President Truman declared himself in favor of a partition scheme proposed, from Paris, by David Ben-Gurion and other Jewish Agency leaders who had escaped the British roundup. Exasperated, Bevin explained his reason for rejecting the plan: "The Arabs won't accept partition. Am I to force it on them with British bayonets?"

Even now, Bevin was still hoping for a negotiated settlement. As a good-will gesture, the imprisoned Jewish Agency leaders were released and a batch of illegal immigrants who had been detained in Cyprus were admitted to Palestine. Something of the same spirit of conciliation appeared at the Zionist Congress of December 1946. Weizmann made a powerful speech warning

2

delegates of the dangers of violence: "If you think of bringing the redemption nearer by un-Jewish methods, if you lose faith in hard work and better days, then you commit idolatry and endanger what we have built . . . 'Zion shall be redeemed in Judgement' — and not by any other means."

But it was too late. There was no proposal the British could make that would gain even grudging acceptance from both the Jews and the Arabs. And Weizmann, although revered as the Grand Old Man of Zionism, had long since passed the mantle of real leadership to others — notably Ben-Gurion — who were determined that redemption would be brought about by whatever means were necessary.

In February 1947, the despairing British referred the whole problem to the United Nations. A U.N. Special Commission on Palestine (UNSCOP) was set up. In a majority report, published on September 1, it recommended the partition of the country into a small Jewish state, a larger Arab state and an internationally administered Jerusalem. The Jews accepted the report. The Arabs and the British did not.

The British wanted out. In addition to being the targets of a ruthless terrorist campaign, they were also incurring worldwide odium for their treatment of those who had survived the Nazi Holocaust. Now, even "in the absence of a settlement," as the colonial secretary put it, Britain "had to plan for an early withdrawal of British forces and of the British administration from Palestine."

In November, the UNSCOP proposals were accepted by the U.N. General Assembly in a modified form that meant more territory for the Arabs. The Americans and Russians, in a rare display of unanimity, both voted in favor. Even in its new form, the plan was again accepted by the Jews and again rejected by the Arabs and the British.

The future of Palestine, however, was no longer in the hands of the diplomats — if, indeed, it ever had been. When news of the assembly's decision reached the Palestinian Arabs, they immediately went on the rampage, killing, burning and looting from one end of the country to the other. The Haganah, which the British had systematically been trying to suppress for months, took time to mobilize. Meanwhile, Jewish casualties mounted. And the British, to their discredit, did little to stop the violence. In many cases, troops and police stood idly by while the rioting went on; more than once, the guardians of law and order openly expressed their approval.

Even at an official level, there was little attempt made at neutrality. The Haganah, desperately short of weapons, was subjected to constant harassment and arms searches. Illegal Jewish immigrants — and potential Haganah recruits — were turned away by the Royal Navy, while armed Arab bands entered the country unmolested from Syria. As one British officer wrote later, "With the machinery of the Palestine government still in position, with officials still going to their offices every morning, with the police in the streets and a considerable army still in its barracks, raging battles were going on in the country unhindered." In December, amidst the chaos, the British announced that they would terminate the mandate on May 15, 1948.

For the Jews, the early months of the struggle were the most critical. The Haganah clung desperately to every scrap of Jewish territory, expending its greatest effort in sending supply convoys through Arab ambushes to outlying settlements and, above all, to the isolated Jewish community in Jerusalem. The greatest problem was lack of arms, and the chief of Britain's Imperial Gen-

Israel's first prime minister, David Ben-Gurion, relaxes in 1961 at the desert kibbutz of Sede Boker. Two years later, the principal architect of Israeli independence retired from active politics; he spent the remaining 10 years of his life here.

eral Staff, Field Marshal Sir Bernard (later Lord) Montgomery, was not alone in believing that the Jews had "bought it." But a shipment of arms purchased from Czechoslovakia — with Russian approval — arrived in March and turned the balance.

However, the Jews now found themselves threatened from a completely unexpected quarter. In the United States, Chaim Weizmann had worked tirelessly to win the support of President Truman, and he seemed to have succeeded. But the American oil lobby, with its increasing interests in the Middle East, had been applying powerful pressure on the State Department to adopt a pro-Arab policy. In the same fateful month of March, the Americans suddenly switched course.

The American ambassador to the United Nations called for a suspension of the partition plan and suggested a temporary United Nations trusteeship over Palestine, "without prejudice to the character of the eventual political settlement." Weizmann addressed a last plea to the White House: "The choice before us, Mr. President, is between statehood and extermination." President Truman, embarrassed by the U.S. turnabout, made Weizmann a promise. If a Jewish state were proclaimed, he told him, he would recognize it immediately.

There was little time to waste. The fighting in Palestine was becoming steadily more bitter. It was a war of populations, not just of soldiers, and the front line ran through every town and village. By the last week of April, 300,000 Arabs had left the country. But beyond its frontiers, the armies of five Arab nations were waiting only for the British to quit before they invaded.

At 9 a.m. on May 14, the last British high commissioner left Palestine. A day ahead of schedule, the mandate was over. And so it was that at 4 p.m. on the same day, David Ben-Gurion read Israel's proclamation of independence to Jewish leaders gathered in the Tel Aviv Museum of Modern Art. (Various names had been suggested for the new state, including Judaea, Zion and Eretz Israel — Land of Israel. The vote had been in favor of Ben-Gurion's suggestion: Israel.) Truman kept his word. He immediately gave the new state provisional but effective recognition; and the Soviet Union followed within hours with full *de jure* recognition.

After almost 2,000 years, the Jews had finally reclaimed the Promised Land. The problem now was whether they would be able to defend it. □

Jubilant crowds in Tel Aviv celebrate the November 9, 1947, United Nations vote in favor of an independent Jewish State in Palestine. When the British withdrew in May 1948, Israel was invaded by neighboring Arabs and a full-scale war broke out.

With his bicycle — a favorite mode of kibbutz transportation — propped near-by, an elderly resident takes his turn at the gate. Every kibbutz has its small guardhouse, but today, it is often less a security measure than a symbol of the community's traditional watchfulness.

THE SELF-CONTAINED WORLD OF THE KIBBUTZ

Each week, in a small settlement on Israel's Mediterranean coast, 500 men and women crowd into their communal dining hall to vote on issues ranging from their children's education to family clothing budgets. They are kibbutzniks, members of one of several hundred agricultural and industrial collectives scattered throughout the country from the Golan Heights in the north to the southern reaches of the Negev. Whether they pick avocados in the kibbutz's orchards, manage its plastics factory or change diapers in its nursery, all kibbutzniks share equally in the ownership of the commune, which provides for their material and social needs from infancy to old age.

With only 3.5 percent of the population living this communal life, the kibbutz movement's contributions to Israeli society far surpass its size. As well as producing nearly half of the nation's agricultural exports, the kibbutzim turn out a high proportion of its political and military leaders: In the Six Day War, for example, nearly one quarter of all army officers were kibbutzniks.

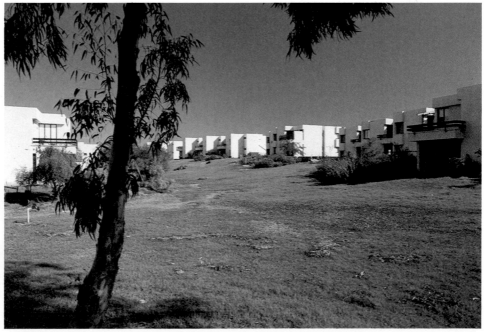

The kibbutz's newest housing — white concrete buildings, each divided into four apartments — provides familes with balcony views across a grassy meadow. On this kibbutz, living space is allocated according to seniority and the size of the families.

RESIDENTS AND WORKING GUESTS

The afternoon sun warms kibbutz volunteers (*below*), as well as drying their towels. Young people from around the world work on the collective for periods from one month to one year, performing unskilled jobs in return for room and board, some pocket money and a taste of communal living.

Having devoted half their day to labor with the kibbutzniks, students in the collective's intensive Hebrew course are given a lesson on the grass. Many collectives have residential language programs, permitting new immigrants and tourists — non-Jews as well as Jews — to learn Hebrew together.

After putting in a day's work that begins at dawn, a husband and wife still find time to read and play with their young children. Families decorate their modest, comfortable apartments according to their own tastes, but their budget for furnishings is determined by an allowance from the community.

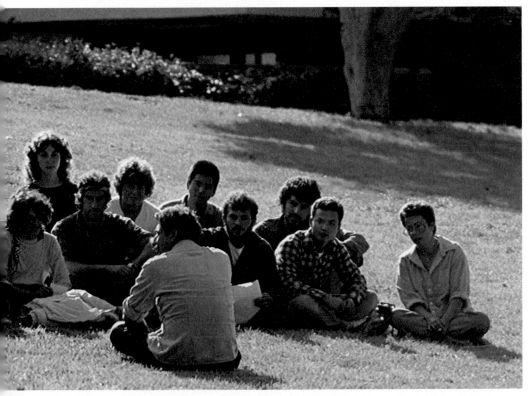

A cafeteria-style meal brings kibbutz-niks and their visitors together in the communal dining hall, the collective's largest building. Although their apartments are equipped with small kitchens, members of the kibbutz prefer the lively bustle of the hall for most meals.

Brightly dressed toddlers wait for their kibbutz child-care worker to ferry them around the commune in an infant cart. This kibbutz — unlike some — allows children to sleep in their parents' home, but beginning in infancy and continuing through high school, youngsters spend their days together.

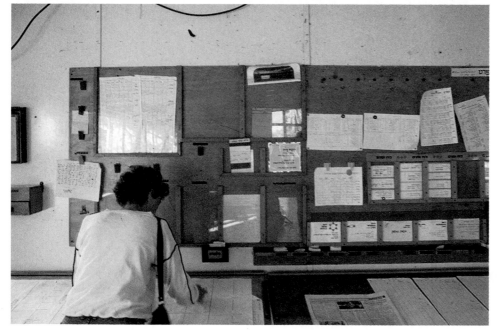

Below a bulletin board displaying information and messages for residents, a woman checks the weekly roster for her job assignment. While the kibbutzim support equality of the sexes, women still predominate in the traditional female domains of kitchen and nursery.

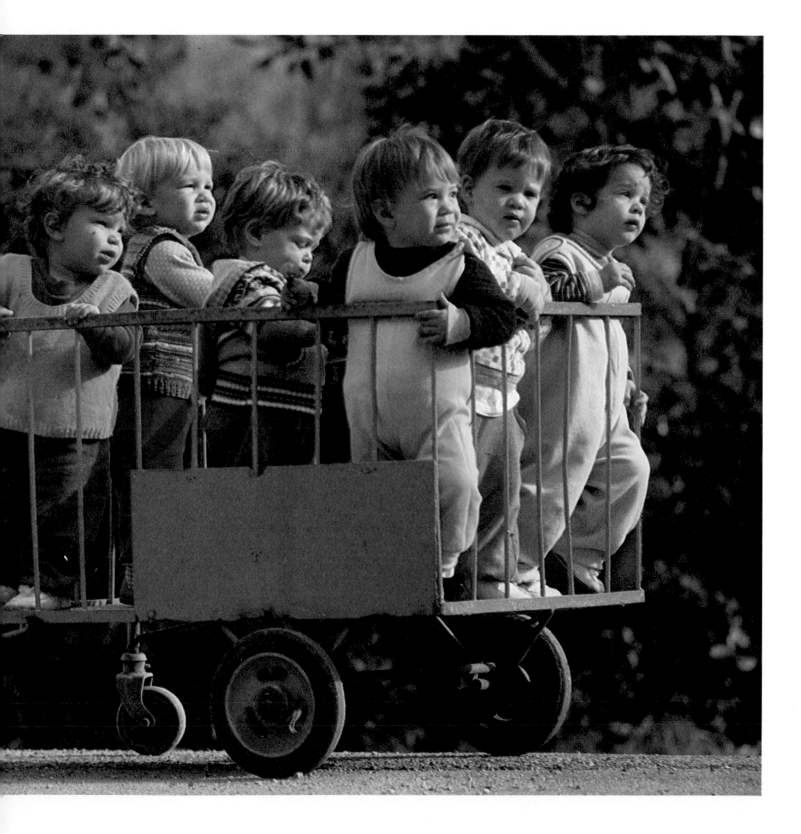

SHARED EFFORT FOR SHARED WEALTH

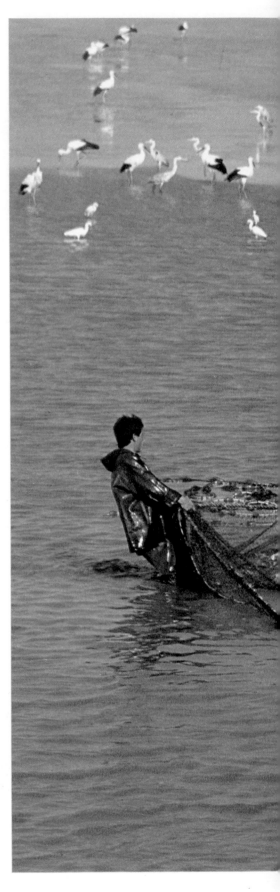

In one of the 50 man-made ponds on the kibbutz, fresh-water fish gathered in nets are sucked out through a yellow vacuum tube for sorting and packing. Because many of its first members were fishers by trade, this commune took up fish farming to provide them with work close to home.

Kibbutz workers tend a banana grove, where blue plastic wrappings protect the fruit from frosts and birds. Begun primarily as agricultural collectives, kibbutzim today have diversified economies: Some 80 percent of this particular collective's wealth comes from the manufacture of plastics.

74

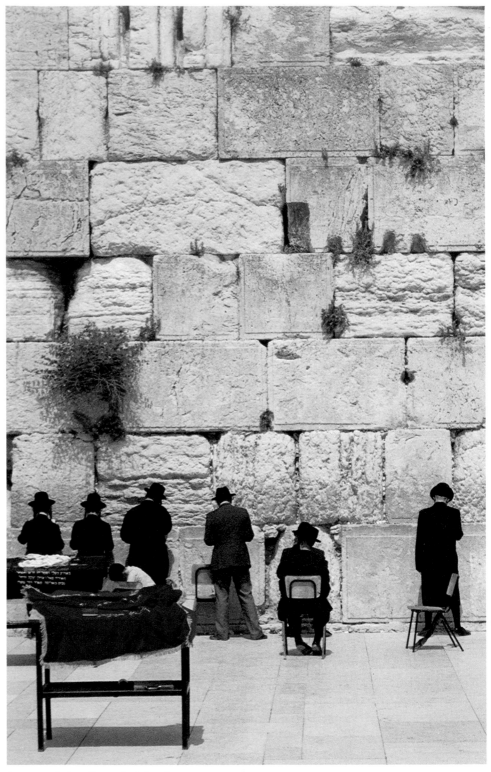

A group of pious Jews, their heads covered in accordance with ancient custom, worship behind prayer tables at Jerusalem's Western Wall. The 52-yard-long wall is the last remnant of the Second Temple, destroyed by the Romans in 70 A.D., and is cherished as a symbol of national survival.

THE MAKING OF AN ISRAELI

It is early evening in Israel. In Tel Aviv's Mann Auditorium, viola player Rachel Kam and her fellow members of the Israel Philharmonic Orchestra wait for the conductor to lead them in a Mozart symphony. Down at the northern edge of the Negev, in the town of Sederot, factory worker Yonathan Angel, his Polish wife, Eliana, and their three sons have finished the evening meal and are listening to Gershwin's *Porgy and Bess* on their French-made stereo. His Sederot neighbors and co-workers — Iraqis, Tunisians, Kurds and Eastern Europeans — are studying their coupons for the state-run Sportoto lottery, working out the best odds for winning a spectacular cash prize.

In a courtyard in Jerusalem, several pale young men in the velour hats and long black coats of an 18th-century Polish ghetto dispute a point of scripture. Up the coast, in a Haifa cake shop, a table of elderly Germans consume *Apfelstrudel* and argue about Marx and Freud. Meanwhile, on a kibbutz in Galilee, the 18-year-old daughter of Canadian immigrants is packing a suitcase for her first stint in the army.

At first glance there seems nothing unusual about this mosaic of lifestyles and origins. Many Western nations have populations almost as varied. But the very ordinariness of the scene is itself extraordinary. It is evidence that for the first time in 2,000 years, Jews — history's perennial outcasts and wanderers — are at last free to live together in a homeland of their own.

Slightly more than one quarter of the world's Jewish population now resides in Israel. The 3.5 million Jewish citizens, or their recent ancestors, have come from 70 different countries, speaking 90 different languages. Yet within this rich ethnic mix, the Moroccan factory worker, the painter of Rumanian parentage, the pop star from Yemen, the kibbutz farmer descended from early Zionist pioneers, the newly arrived American physicist and the shopkeeper whose forebears have clung tenaciously to the place since the Middle Ages all feel equally at home.

But this powerful sense of belonging did not come to pass overnight. The founders of the state realized that the transformation of newcomers from many different lands into seasoned citizens would be a complex and continuous process. Being Jewish, even being a Zionist — ideologically committed to Jewish settlement in Israel — would not be common ground enough. It would take time, effort and a subtle chemistry to imbue people from such diverse backgrounds with a shared sense of nationhood. The Jews may be an ancient people, but Israel is a young country; the first generation born into citizenship is only now entering middle age.

Many different factors have been at work in the conversion of Jews into Israelis. The first is, inevitably, Zionism itself. The first Jewish settlers in Palestine, and many of their present-day successors, came to the land with the aspiration of reconstructing a Jewish state in the ancient homeland of the Hebrew people. It is difficult for non-Jews, particularly those who have al-ways been part of an ethnic majority and have never suffered persecution or discrimination, to realize the passion with which some Jews regard the opportunity of living in Israel. Yonathan Angel's view is typical of many Israelis: "A Jew can only be a proud Jew by living here." In modern Hebrew, the process of emigrating and settling in Israel is called *Aliya,* or "Ascending"; new immigrants are called *olim,* meaning "those who go up." Not all Jews are Zionists, but those who are perceive the move to Israel, quite literally, as an elevation to a higher mode of life.

Others come, not out of idealism, but in desperation. Before World War II, the last wave of immigrants to Palestine were refugees from Nazi rule. After the war and in the first few years of independence, the first influx of new arrivals were survivors from the Nazi Holocaust, pouring out of the Displaced Persons camps of postwar Europe. They had nowhere else to go.

Musician Rachel Kam's parents, for instance, arrived in Israel after years as refugees. Her father, uprooted from his home in southern Poland, joined a band of Russian partisans fighting the Nazis. Her blue-eyed Lithuanian-born mother saved herself from the concentration camps with a set of false papers declaring her to be of Aryan race; she spent the war years working as a housemaid in the German city of Stuttgart, terrified that her deception would be uncovered. The couple met after the end of the war at a Displaced Persons camp in Italy, married and entered Palestine as part of a shipload of illegal im-

3

migrants defying the British blockade.

Hard on the heels of the Holocaust refugees came the mass emigrations of Jews from Arab lands. In 1949 and 1950, some 50,000 Yemenites — virtually the entire Jewish population of that country — trekked on foot or on mule-back through the Arabian mountains to the British colony of Aden, where they were transported to Israel in a carefully organized airlift, Operation *Magic Carpet*. A few months later, Operation *Ezra and Nehemiah* ferried 150,000 Jews out of Iraq via Cyprus to Israel.

The 1950s and early 1960s saw a succession of lulls and peaks in the inflow of new citizens, as well as the emigration of some who had decided that the grass was, after all, greener in the lands of exile. The 1956 clash between Israel and Egypt in the Sinai peninsula brought 14,500 Egyptian Jews to Israel, while 85,000 Jewish North Africans

from the newly independent and increasingly nationalist states of Morocco and Tunisia opted for *Aliya* during the same period. Refugees from political disturbances in Poland and from the 1956 Hungarian revolution swelled the numbers of European arrivals.

In the 1960s, fewer settlers came from those areas known in Israel as "the lands of stress," and more came from the affluent urban areas of North and South America, Britain and South Africa. Typical of these immigrants is Sara Ben-Menachem, born in Argentina but now a dentist in Jerusalem. As the daughter of a prosperous industrialist, she had a comfortable life in Buenos Aires. In 1961, her family sent her to Israel to fetch back a sister who, to their chagrin, wished to settle there. "My parents were Zionists," she recalled, "but Zionists who did not want to live in Palestine." As soon as she ar-

rived, she felt that the Jewish state, not South America, was where she belonged. "I couldn't convince my sister to return. In fact, I liked Israel so much that I stayed myself. I felt at home here, and now Israel is my place. For better or worse. . . ."

The Six Day War in 1967 proved to be a watershed. Young people from the West flocked to Israel as volunteers, to serve as army auxiliaries, construction workers, medical aides and social workers, freeing more Israelis for the war. Afterward, many of them stayed on, spearheading another increase in immigration and coinciding with a concerted effort by the Israeli government and the World Zionist Organization to encourage new settlement.

In the early 1970s, Israel received 45,000 Soviet Jews, the first wave of those who had struggled long and hard for permission to emigrate to Israel.

HOUSING AN INFLUX OF IMMIGRANTS

Between 1949 and 1984, about 1.75 million immigrants arrived in Israel. They came from widely different backgrounds: Some were displaced persons from the refugee camps of postwar Europe, others were from Argentina or South Africa, Iraq or Yemen. From the moment of independence in 1948, homes had to be built in great numbers and at high speed; new villages rose rapidly, and although the buildings were often just temporary huts, they did offer lodging for tens of thousands.

Today, 40 absorption centers throughout the country aid newcomers. Here, trained staff and interpreters teach basic Hebrew, offer films and lectures on Israeli society and, above all, give guidance on finding jobs and housing and on coping with bureaucracy.

In a photograph from the 1950s, Moroccan Jews arrive at their state-built homes in Galilee.

Emigration, whatever the destination, is not a right normally accorded to any Soviet citizen; for Jews the situation has been particularly difficult. Because of their government's unfriendliness toward Israel, those who still identify as Jews are regarded with suspicion. They feel themselves to be more severely repressed than other religious or cultural minorities in the U.S.S.R. Their campaign for permission to emigrate to Israel has gained widespread sympathy in the West, although it has been only partially successful. The would-be emigrants, including many professionals and academics, cannot always afford the punitive "exit tax," which is imposed to recoup the state's investment in their education and training.

But not all Soviet emigrants are doctors, scientists or musicians. Thousands of members of highly religious, inward-looking Jewish communities from Soviet Asia have also made *Aliya*, coming from Georgia, Bokhara and villages in the Caucasus mountains. Once settled in Israel, they tend to remain within their own communities, living in large extended families and preserving their own deeply pious way of life.

Soviet Jews do not all find fulfillment in the Promised Land. Once out of the U.S.S.R., some who manage to obtain exit visas settle elsewhere in the West. And a few will return to their native country, unable to adapt to an alien, noncommunist environment or disillusioned by the gap between their expectations and Israeli reality.

The 1970s and 1980s brought several thousand African newcomers: black Ethiopian Jews known as the Falashas, the "Strangers." They are thought by some scholars to have derived from the ancient Israelite tribe of Dan. Living in remote mountainous regions, they were completely cut off from the Jewish mainstream; indeed, until the end of the 19th century, they believed that all Jews were black. They retained customs that the rest of the Jewish world had long abandoned, such as animal sacrifice, and used an ancient Ethiopic dialect instead of Hebrew as their liturgical language. Although they possessed the Torah — the Five Books of Moses — they had no knowledge of later religious texts, such as the Talmud.

When Ethiopia was devastated by famine in the early 1980s, the trickle of Ethiopian emigrants turned into a well-publicized flood. Some 7,500 were evacuated to Israel in 1984 by a covert and politically controversial airlift called Operation *Moses*. Nations unfriendly to Israel condemned it as a propaganda ploy, while Israelis defended their action as a bold attempt to rescue their people from a war-torn land that could no longer feed them.

"We can only gain from showing the world the extent to which we are willing to go to rescue Jews," said one Israeli official. "This mission is a national achievement of the highest order."

In a world where many states are eager to restrict immigration by rewriting their laws and devising legal loopholes to keep people out, Israel may well be unique in its efforts to encourage and assist new arrivals. There is, however, a crucial condition: Israel's doors are open, but only Jews have the automatic right to Israeli citizenship. The 1948 Declaration of Independence proclaimed: "The State of Israel shall be open to Jewish immigration and the ingathering of the exiles." Two years after independence, the Knesset, Israel's Parliament, passed the 1950 Law of Return, granting every Jew the right of

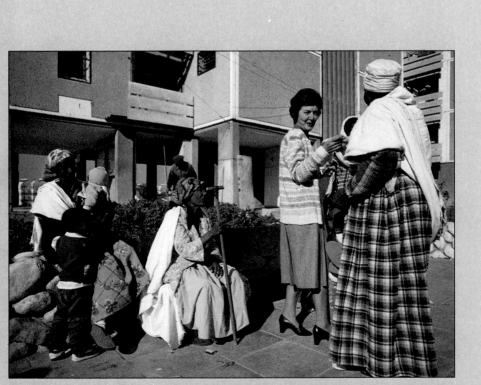

The director of a Beersheba absorption center stops for a chat with Ethiopian newcomers.

permanent settlement in Israel. In 1954 a statute was enacted entitling all Jewish immigrants to citizenship as soon as they set foot on Israeli soil.

This Right of Return continues to generate controversy. According to religious law, a person may be defined as a Jew if he or she is the child of a Jewish mother, or a convert who has adopted Judaism after a prescribed course of study and a ritual conversion process carried out by a rabbi. But a small and vocal minority within the Israeli religious establishment questions the identity of groups such as the Ethiopians, whose origins and traditions differ from those of other Jews. It was not until 1973, after much acrimonious debate over the first Ethiopian arrivals, that they were officially acknowledged as Jews by the religious establishment. Some rabbis demanded they undergo a form of symbolic conversion ceremony to confirm their Jewishness. Not surprisingly, the Ethiopians, who feel their own ritual purity far exceeds that of most Israelis, indignantly refused.

Non-Jews may also apply for naturalization, but they have no automatic entitlement to citizenship. Even some members of the Jewish faith no longer enjoy the undisputed right to an Israeli passport. It was discovered that certain Jewish criminals, or those with strong underworld associations, experienced sudden bursts of Zionist fervor when they felt the hot breath of the law on their necks. In 1972, for instance, New Yorker Meyer Lansky, worried by the attentions of an American grand jury, was denied the right of permanent residence in Israel. His unsuccessful lawsuit against the government was one of a number of test cases that reinforced the Minister of the Interior's right to withhold an immigrant's visa from "a person with a criminal past, likely to endanger the public welfare."

For law-abiding citizens who wish to move to Israel, the path is made smoother by the Jewish Agency of the autonomous World Zionist Organization. The Agency maintains offices in countries with substantial Jewish populations, staffed by Israeli counselors — *shlichim,* or "messengers" — who provide guidance and help for prospective immigrants.

In some cases, several like-minded people will decide to emigrate together. A group of young Americans or Canadians, for instance, with a common philosophy of life and shared political or religious opinions, will form a *garin* — a settlement group of perhaps 10 families — and pool their resources to establish a new kibbutz. They will negotiate with the Ministry of the Interior for permission to settle in an undeveloped area, then live in trailers until permanent dwellings can be built. Or a party of engineers and scientists may decide to create a new community within commuting distance of Israel's high-tech industries.

More often, however, individuals come to Israel singly or in families and spend their first few months in the Jewish Agency's residential hostels and Absorption Centers. Here they study the Hebrew language and acclimate themselves to life in a new country. Trained staff are on hand to assist them in job- and house-hunting and to guide them through the labyrinths of the Israeli bureaucracy. It takes patience, persistence and a level head to acquire identity cards, health insurance and the numerous tax concessions and benefits that are available only to newcomers; civil servants operate an intricate system that retains elements of imperial

3

Ottoman law and British Mandatory practices, with newer Israeli regulations grafted on top.

Zionism may provide the impetus for settlement, and the absorption services may offer newcomers the resources to make themselves at home in their adopted country; but since the beginning of the state there has been no agency as powerful as the Israeli Defense Forces for turning immigrants into Israelis. All new residents, male and female, are liable for conscription under the same terms and conditions as native-born Israelis.

Because the nation was born out of war, the first immigrants to the newly established nation had little option but to join in the collective battle for survival. During the 1948-1949 War of Independence all hands were needed, and it was not unknown for an immigrant to become an Israeli citizen and an Israeli casualty on the same day. But once the war was over, the founders of the nation felt it was possible for the army to play a more pacific and constructive role. "The army," observed David Ben-Gurion, "is obliged to become the creative force of the nation's pioneers and the cultural instrument for the assimilation of returnees, for their integration and their advancement."

The Defense Service Law of 1949 established the foundation for the key educational role of the military establishment. Under the terms of this law, the army was mandated to teach conscripts the Hebrew language, Bible studies, Israeli and general history, geography, science and other disciplines. Today its three-month courses in these subjects, equipped with special textbooks, provide an intensive 200 hours of instruction aimed at bringing every

recruit up to the minimum basic educational standard. It is probably the only military organization in the world that has won a national prize for contributions to education.

By Western standards, Israel's army is unconventional in many other ways. Enlisted men and women are often on familiar first-name terms with their officers, they share the same rations and eat in the same mess, and — in times of peace, at least — they feel free to argue with their superiors rather than obey orders unquestioningly.

Women in the army perform a wide range of noncombat roles but, to the frustration of some female soldiers, they are no longer sent to the front lines. Indeed, Israeli feminists have pointed out that although women and men are equally liable to conscription, women have more opportunities for avoiding their military service and — if enlisted — are more restricted in their choice of role than their counterparts in, for instance, the United States Army. However, women soldiers are trained for combat so that they can be used extensively as technical instructors. It is common on Israeli military bases to see a 19-year-old female sergeant drilling a platoon of reservists old enough to be her father, and to see young women officers teaching conscripts on machine guns or tanks.

Both women and men are trained with equal rigor for the elite units of the NAHAL. NAHAL — a Hebrew acronym for Fighting Pioneer Youth — is a part of the Israeli Defense Forces (IDF) with the mission of forming and maintaining armed agricultural settlements and kibbutzim in the sensitive border areas. Its members are instructed in the skills of farming as well as fighting, and they spend their enlisted time liv-

ing and working in these communities.

Most Israelis look upon their military service as an obligation to the community. But there are, as in every country, those who would prefer to avoid conscription. Women are exempted from service if they are married or if they declare themselves to be highly religious; it is accepted that the traditional codes of dress and conduct for a pious Jewish woman are incompatible with the demands of military life. However, one young woman who had obtained an exemption on grounds of her extreme piety was spotted a week later taking part in the Miss Tel Aviv contest, clad in the briefest of bikinis; she was instantly hustled into the army.

The Israeli man without a military record carries a stigma for the rest of his life, so some young men go to extreme lengths to gain entry. A military doctor in Jerusalem remarked, "We are probably the only army medics in the world who find ourselves trying to detect sick boys who claim to be healthy, rather than the other way around."

Yudin Ya'akov, a young would-be recruit, was turned down by the IDF because of poor hearing. Since his disability was not apparent, he became the subject of malicious gossip among his neighbors, who accused him of shirking his duties. Frustrated, Ya'akov sued the army, claiming that his impaired hearing did not make him unfit for service and that his rejection had caused him "unjustifiable shame and brought disgrace" upon his family. The Supreme Court upheld his claim and ordered that he be inducted at once.

In spite of its risks and perils, military service brings concrete rewards to the veteran, providing specialist qualifications, financial benefits, and an enormous pool of social and professional

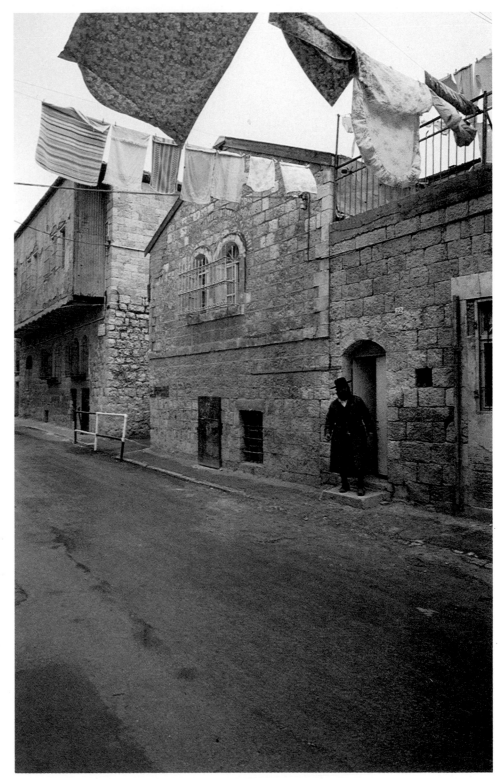

contacts. In the army, Israelis of different ethnic backgrounds, generations and social classes get to know one another; barriers of ignorance and prejudice are inevitably broken down. Because the IDF touches the lives of the overwhelming majority — native-born and newcomers alike — it may well be the one Israeli institution that can truly claim to be a melting pot.

After only decades of independence, Israel is still a nation in flux, a society very much in its infancy. Without the inheritance of a continuous common culture and a shared history played out in a single place, Israelis are engrossed in the process of inventing and defining their own national identity.

The Hebrew language, adapted by Zionist scholars for modern use, has been a cohesive force. Once immigrants have learned the language, they often express a desire for assimilation by changing their names into something that sounds more Hebraic. It is probably easier to change a name legally in Israel than anywhere else, and 80 percent of Israelis have seen fit to do so. By filling in a short form and paying a nominal fee at the government office, a citizen is instantly transformed. Within minutes, a woman with the Arabic-Jewish name of Toria Sa'id, for instance, becomes the far more Israeli-sounding Nurit Shimoni.

The precedent was set long before independence: The early Zionist settlers felt it was one way of proving their resolve to build new lives in a new country. A young Russian Jew named David Grien, for instance, emigrated to Palestine and became David Ben-Gurion. Succeeding prime ministers have done the same: Moshe Shertok became Sharett, Levi Shkolnick became Levi Eshkil,

In a religious ecstasy, male members of the Hasidic sect swirl inside a Mea Shearim synagogue while one of their number claps out a rhythm. The circular dance symbolizes a Hasidic precept: No one leads, no one follows, all are equal before God.

3

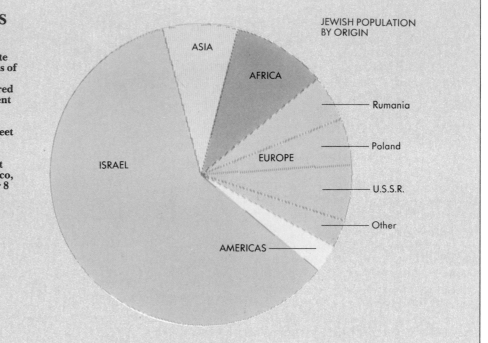

PEOPLE OF DIVERSE ORIGINS

Jewish immigration began long before the state of Israel was founded. In the 1880s, thousands of Jews, fleeing anti-Semitic pogroms in Poland and Russia, poured into Palestine. One hundred years later, Jews accounted for about 83 percent of Israel's population.

Of these Jewish inhabitants 60 percent are Israeli-born — nicknamed sabras after the sweet but prickly fruit of the common cactus; 19 percent came from Europe, mainly from Rumania, Poland and the U.S.S.R.; 10 percent are African, the majority coming from Morocco, Algeria, Tunisia and Egypt; Asia accounts for 8 percent — mostly Iraqis, Iranians and Turks; while another 3 percent were born in the Americas or Australia.

JEWISH POPULATION BY ORIGIN

ASIA — AFRICA — Rumania — Poland — EUROPE — U.S.S.R. — Other — ISRAEL — AMERICAS

Golda Myerson opted for the more Hebraic surname of Meir.

Just as individuals take new names to reflect their new nationality, so the Israeli authorities have created new place names to put a Hebrew stamp on the map. In part, the creation of new names reflects the creation of new places: Some 1,000 kibbutzim, villages and development towns have been established since the first waves of Zionist settlement, 650 since independence. A Names Committee, composed of specialists in archeology, history, geography, folklore and ancient Hebrew, meets regularly to consider names for these fledgling communities.

First set up in 1924 by the Jewish Agency, the committee became a government body after statehood. It has named more than 889 locations, often reviving place names mentioned in the Bible or the Talmud.

A new settlement in the Hebron hills, for instance, was named Othniel, after one of the judges who presided over the tribes of Israel in the time of Joshua — the 12th century B.C. — who was known to have lived in the district.

Even when the Scriptures supply no specific geographical or historical association, they may still be used as sources of inspiration. Faced with the task of naming three rural villages in the northern Negev and the new town that would serve them as a regional center, the committee looked to an Old Testament verse, Isaiah 41:19: "I will plant in the wilderness . . . the fig tree, and the pine and the box tree, together." The villages were called by the Hebrew words for the trees — Berosh, Tidhar and Ta'ashur — while the central town was named Yahdav, or "Together."

Other new communities have more recent associations. The committee has named settlements after figures from modern Jewish history — Herzliyya, for example, commemorates the founding father of Zionism, Theodor Herzl — and after military heroes: A settlement in the Jordan Valley called Netiv Halamed-heh (The Thirty-Five) perpetuates the memory of 35 soldiers who fell there. Non-Jewish supporters of the state are similarly honored: The kibbutz of Ramat David is named for the former British prime minister David Lloyd George, an early supporter of the Zionist cause, and Kfar Truman for

84

the American president who urged the United Nations to approve an independent Israeli state.

"Instead of erecting a statue in the park," explained one committee member, "we prefer to award friends of our nation a living memorial, and name a settlement after them."

It is not surprising that a state whose claim to its territory is still questioned by some should be so zealous in reinforcing its people's long-standing connection with the land. But this concern is practical as well as political. Older nations take their heroes, legends and patriotic symbols for granted, as part of their cultural heritage, but a new society needs to invent them afresh.

For the so-called "People of the Book," it is natural that the Bible

should be the principal source for this imagery. During his term as Israel's first prime minister, David Ben-Gurion insisted that the study of the Bible — as geography, history and literature rather than as holy writ — be made an integral part of the school curriculum, to give the rising generation a positive Jewish-Israeli identity.

For the same reason, objects from Jewish history were chosen as national symbols. The six-pointed star known as the Star of David was placed on the Israeli flag, and the Menora — a seven-branched candelabra revered as a reminder of the ancient temple — became the official state emblem and the insignia of the Israeli Defense Forces.

Places also take on symbolic significance. The Western Wall in Jerusalem

is the sole surviving remnant of the Second Temple, and it is a site charged with a sense of history and national sentiment. So, too, is Masada, on its lonely rock in the Judaean desert. Here, where 960 Jewish resistance fighters — men, women and children — committed suicide in 73 A.D. rather than yield to Roman besiegers, new recruits to the IDF's elite Armored Corps take their oath of allegiance, vowing that "Masada shall not fall again."

Horrors more recent than a Roman siege have burned the promise "Never Again" even deeper into the Israeli soul. The somber monument of Yad Vashem (the name means "hand" and "name") in Jerusalem is dedicated to the six million Jews — more than one third of the world's Jewish popula-

3

tion — who died at Nazi hands. Here, historical archives — photographic records of concentration-camp atrocities and memorial plaques to European Jewish communities that were wiped out — are preserved to ensure Israelis never forget, never grow complacent.

The Holocaust has profound implications for all Israelis, whether of European or Afro-Asian origin. But after 2,000 years of dispersion, Jews from different regions have different histories; they are no longer, if they ever were, one homogeneous ethnic group.

Relations between Ashkenazic Jews, who originate in the Yiddish-speaking communities of Central and Eastern Europe, and Jews of Oriental and North African extraction have not always been easy. The latter are known, imprecisely, as Sephardim, after Sepharad — the ancient Hebrew name for Spain. Strictly speaking, Sephardim are those who can trace their ancestry back to the large Jewish communities that flourished in Spain during the Middle Ages, but in Israeli parlance the term is often used to distinguish those Jews who are of Afro-Asian — as opposed to European — stock.

When the state was first founded, the Ashkenazim were in the majority. Now, after waves of immigration from the Arab world and a consistently higher birth rate, the Sephardim form just over half of the Jewish population.

Each group has its rich and poor, its proletarians, peasants and urban cosmopolites. But for the first three decades of the state's existence, Jews from North Africa and Yemen — who came from economically and educationally deprived backgrounds — were clustered in the most underprivileged sectors of Israeli society. Despite its egali-

tarian ideals, the nation appeared, for a time, to be moving toward an ethnically based class system.

From the beginning, Ashkenazic Jews were firmly in control of the establishment, occupying the prime jobs, enjoying the best housing and running the government. Many Afro-Asian immigrants remained at the bottom of the ladder, living in slums and working in poorly paid menial jobs. Because of their higher birth rate, they suffered disproportionately from overcrowded and inadequate housing. In schools, their children often displayed the problems associated with a background of poverty and multiple deprivation: They failed more subjects, dropped out of school earlier, and fell into petty crime at a rate far greater than their more privileged contemporaries.

Inevitably, frustration in these communities mounted. In 1971, a group of young Jews of Middle Eastern origin, angry at what they saw as official indifference to their plight, formed a protest movement. They named it the Black Panthers, drawing a parallel between their own struggle and that of black militants in the U.S. They staged angry and sometimes violent demonstrations in the cities; some were jailed. Prime Minister Golda Meir, after receiving an angry delegation of them in 1972, sent them away with the remark, "These are not nice boys."

But the government was not complacent. The Ministry of Education instituted policies to integrate poor and middle-class school children, to break the vicious cycle of deprived children in deprived schools in deprived neighborhoods. The package of education reforms and financial assistance included grants to aid large families, provision of extra tutoring, and the creation of re-

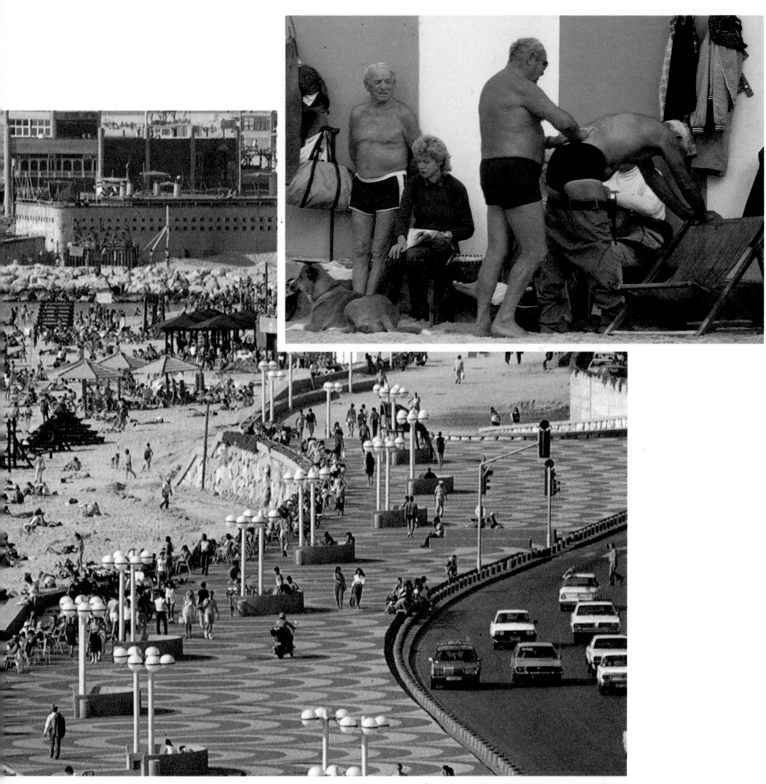

On the beachfront in Tel Aviv, within sight of the city's marina, Israelis stroll along the decorative promenade of Hayarkon Street, sunbathe, or swim in the Mediterranean Sea. In front of one of the blue-and-white changing booths *(inset)*, an elderly man rubs suntan lotion onto a friend's back.

3

medial and enrichment programs to improve students' chances of qualifying for higher education.

The state has also poured massive resources into welfare services and housing, while Israel's central trade union organization, the Histadrut, has guaranteed all workers the right to equal pay and promotion prospects. Economic inequities and housing problems take time to rectify, but the gulf does appear to be narrowing at last.

Material improvements do not automatically put an end to intercommunal tensions. Many Israelis of Afro-Asian origin feel that they have been written out of the nation's history.

In schools, for instance, they complain that little is said about those settlers who came from Yemen or Iraq at the same time as the early Zionist pioneers from Central and Eastern Europe. Because the latter were politically and culturally dominant, they tended to forget that Afro-Asian Jews had also played a role. "They teach that 'the first *Aliya* was this group' — but where are the Sephardim?" asks one Yemenite university lecturer, a specialist on Jews from Islamic countries.

A North African community leader feels that it is time his own people were appreciated as contributors to Israeli life — not merely as stereotyped purveyors of exotic delicacies or the wearers of picturesque dress. "We want to be recognized not via the couscous and the caftan, but through our writers and poets, through our agricultural achievements and through our willingness to sacrifice ourselves in the line of fire on the nation's borders."

For many Israelis the goal now is to achieve a society that is, at once, heterogeneous and united, ethnically varied but socially equal. Educational and cul-

KOSHER FOOD LAWS

A rabbi holds up a scoop of kosher flour.

The dietary laws of *kashruth* (Hebrew for "right," or "fit"), dictating the food that Jews may or may not eat, originated in the Old Testament. For the citizen of modern Israel, whether to keep kosher or not is a personal matter, but many people do observe the prohibitions against shellfish, pork and certain other meats, and refrain from mixing meat and dairy foods.

Some food producers employ rabbis to ensure that their products conform to the minutely detailed rules of *kashruth*. Flour mills, for example, seek confirmation that the meal used in the making of Passover matzo — unleavened bread — has not fermented.

tural organizations such as Beyahad work toward this end. Founded by North Africans in 1979, it seeks not only to celebrate the contributions made by Afro-Asian Jewry, but to encourage tolerance and mutual appreciation between all Israelis — Oriental and European, Jew and Arab.

One of the most successful of its projects has been the expansion of the traditional North African Jewish spring holiday, Mimouna, into a national celebration. Customarily, North African families treat this two-day festival as an occasion for impromptu, but lavish, hospitality. They open their houses to all their neighbors, offering traditional sweets and mint tea. Under the auspices of Beyahad, Mimouna has become a large-scale public event with vast communal picnics and folk festivals in the parks, open-air exhibitions celebrating the nation's cultural diversity, ceremonial visits by public figures to North African households and an officially sanctioned day off from school. The organizers see the occasion as an opportunity for Israelis of many different backgrounds to begin to understand each other, a way to break down prejudices that still survive.

"We haven't yet reached the stage of respecting one another's cultures," admits founder Sam Ben-Chetrit. But he is optimistic: "Israeli society is more open today than before, more tolerant and prepared to listen. There is a readiness to solve problems."

With increasing frequency, different cultures meet within one household, as the children of immigrants intermarry. One family where two worlds converge is that of Yonathan and Eliana Angel, who live on the northern edge of the Negev, in the town of Sederot.

The Angels' family history is itself an example of the Zionist act of "gathering in the exiles." Both Yonathan and Eliana were born in Israel, but they grew up in two different environments: Yonathan is a Yemenite-Israeli, and Eliana's origins are Polish.

Yonathan — also known as Natti — is olive-skinned, slim, slightly balding. He has a finely sculptured Yemenite face, burning black eyes and slender hands. He wears colorful turtleneck sweaters and jeans, and he never puts on a tie. He speaks in the rhythmic, authentic Hebrew that the Yemenites have preserved since they were exiled from Palestine 2,000 years ago. His father came to Israel as a child, in 1903, as part of

the Yemenites' own *Aliya*. The family spent six months on an arduous trek, sometimes riding on donkeys, sometimes walking, to reach the Red Sea port of Aden. Here they found a boat bound for Palestine. On the journey, the small boy was entrusted with the family's most precious Yemenite heirloom — a magnificent antique silver water pipe, standing more than a yard high — which today adorns the Angels' comfortable living room in Sederot.

Natti himself was born in the city of Petah Tikvah, which lies to the north of Tel Aviv. He remembers that his father walked great distances every day to labor in the citrus plantations outside the city, and that his mother took in laun-

dry to help support the large family.

Following the pattern of many of his contemporaries from deprived backgrounds, Natti dropped out of school in his early teens. He had little ambition or sense of direction. "I was a ne'er-do-well until I met Eliana," he admits.

Fair-skinned, round-faced Eliana Zaidengart comes from another world. She is, like so many Ashkenazim of her generation, a child of the Holocaust: Her father, a medical student, was shipped off to a concentration camp; her mother endured three nightmarish years at Auschwitz. Eliana was born in the port of Jaffa (now part of the municipality of Tel Aviv – Jaffa). In her early teens she moved with her family to Sederot, at the time only a struggling frontier settlement.

When Eliana went back to Tel Aviv to train as a teacher, she met and married Natti and persuaded him to return with her to Sederot. At first, he found the place too quiet.

"I had a hard time adjusting. I was a city boy and here I was cooped up in a village. But I've grown to love it here. We have a close-knit group of friends of our own age — Yemenites, Tunisians, Poles. The tempo is relaxed, and I'm doing well at the plant."

Natti works in a pharmaceuticals factory, making bandages and other surgical products from the locally grown cotton. Eliana teaches kindergarten and runs a cultural-enrichment program for the local schools.

Natti refers to himself as a Yemenite-Israeli and Eliana sees herself as a Polish-Israeli, but their three sons are unmistakably *sabras* — native-born Israeli citizens, nicknamed after the indigenous cactus that is prickly outside, but soft and sweet within.

"It nevers occurs to them or to their friends to question whether they are Ashkenazi or Sephardi," says Eliana. Her husband agrees, and he insists that the children feel no discrimination because their skin is darker or because their father is a Yemenite. "Even I personally did not feel it in my youth, although I realized that the country then was being run by Europeans, and it is natural for the ruling group to favor its own. We all do that — Ashkenazi or Sephardi or Yemenite. Gaps really come from cultural differences. As soon as they are bridged, the gaps disappear. That is one Israeli problem that doesn't worry me."

Sederot, where the Angels live, is one of Israel's 30 development towns, a

meeting place for many different immigrant groups. It was established in 1954 as part of a program of planned settlements. They were intended to distribute the burgeoning population over a wider area and to provide a commercial and industrial base for the growing number of kibbutzim and agricultural cooperatives. Sederot, for instance, has several plants that make use of local crops: a cotton gin, the pharmaceuticals firm where Natti Angel is employed, a poultry-processing factory and a potato-chip manufacturer.

The town's first inhabitants were immigrants from Iraq, Iran and Kurdistan, joined later by Eastern Europeans, North Africans and — even more recently — by Ethiopians.

In the early days, Sederot, like most development towns, was a spartan place, composed mostly of temporary huts and cabins where large families squeezed into one or two small rooms. But these have gradually been replaced by new houses — built mainly by the Arab laborers who commute from Gaza, 12 miles away.

Sephardic Jews, who form the major-

ity in the development town, are traditionally very pious; Sederot boasts 20 synagogues for a population of 10,000, as well as social clubs, shops, and a movie theater that shows first-run European and American films. Buses go to Tel Aviv and Beersheba, a two-hour journey, but there is no local public transportation. People without cars travel by bicycle, horse or foot. Despite light industries and a polyglot population, Sederot remains a small country town, without a single traffic light.

The pace of life outside semirural Sederot is more frenetic. Of Israel's inhabitants, 85 percent are urbanites, most of whom live on the crowded coastal plain: Greater Tel Aviv alone houses 35 percent of the population.

In many ways, the lifestyles of these Israelis do not differ markedly from those of their counterparts elsewhere. But demographically as well as geographically, they are poised between two worlds, not quite a Middle Eastern society, not quite European.

This mingling of cultures is reflected in their favorite pastimes and sports. As

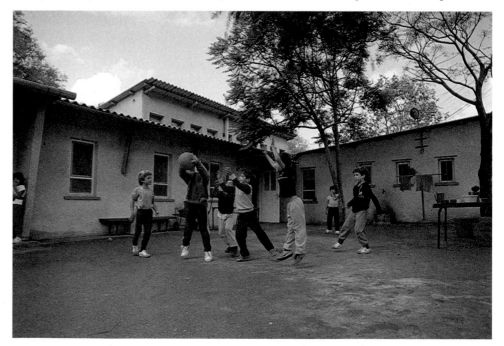

At a kibbutz near Caesarea, young basketball players practice blocking and passing. The sport's popularity skyrocketed when an Israeli team, Maccabi Tel Aviv, achieved international fame by winning a series of European championships.

befits a land with so benign a climate, these pleasures are often enjoyed out of doors. As in other Mediterranean countries, people are forever eating in the streets; food vendors offer everything from Middle Eastern chick-pea fritters to transatlantic hot dogs, and discarded shells of sunflower seeds — a favorite snack — crackle underfoot.

The most popular sports mirror this diversity: Soccer is supported as fanatically in Israel as anywhere in Europe, and an important national match can bring the country virtually to a halt. North American immigrants have imported their devotion to basketball, which has been embraced enthusiastically throughout Israel; one shining star has been a black American convert to Judaism. And the erstwhile British Empire has sent cricketers: Australians, Englishmen and Indians.

Popular culture provides the context for other forms of cross fertilization. The Hebrew-language songs at the top of the pop music charts, for example, amalgamate Arabic, Latin and North American styles. In one respect, Israelis perpetuate the cultural values of the lost world of Central European Jewry: They are passionate devotees of classical music. Israel has a higher percentage of concertgoers than any other country and takes pride in the success of such native sons as violinists Yitzhak Perlman and Pinchas Zukerman and conductor Daniel Barenboim.

Young musicians and other performing artists are carefully nurtured by means of special tutoring, scholarships and youth orchestras. In so small a country, efforts can be made to prevent talent from slipping through the cracks, even if it sometimes means that the rules must be bent a little: "I will not let the army stand in the way of this girl's career as a dancer!" one IDF officer was heard to say, as she ordered a young conscript to go off guard duty in time for rehearsal.

For viola player Rachel Kam, a place in the the Israel Philharmonic Orchestra was the pinnacle of her musical ambition. "For an Israeli kid, the Philharmonic was untouchable."

Thanks to sympathetic teaching and to a scholarship from the same cultural foundation that launched Perlman and Pinchas Zukerman on their careers, she eventually won a place in the orchestra. Now she fits in family life around the IPO's punishing concert schedule — 300 or so concerts a year and foreign tours as far afield as South America and Japan. "We are always well received," she says. "I think the IPO is one of Israel's best ambassadors."

The Israeli Philharmonic Orchestra's distinguished international reputation is, for all Israelis, a matter of patriotic pride. As citizens of a small, young and much-criticized country, they display an almost obsessive need to excel at everything they do.

Yet simpler, more pragmatic hopes for the future go hand in hand with these vaulting ambitions. "I look at my kids," says Rachel Kam, "and I wish for them to be happy in Israel and not to have to fight any more wars, to be content with themselves and to get the best out of every working day." □

WITHIN THE WALLS OF OLD JERUSALEM

Crammed into 250 acres and enclosed by its massive 16th-century walls, the Old City of Jerusalem has a unique importance for three of the world's major religions: Among its jumbled buildings and labyrinthine alleys lie some of the oldest and holiest shrines of each faith.

The Old City, which occupies less than 1 percent of Israel's sprawling capital, consists of four sectors. Built on the spacious platform that was once the site of Solomon's Temple, the Dome of the Rock — Islam's oldest surviving religious monument — rises above the Muslim Quarter. The platform's western revetment is the Western Wall — ancient focus of exiled Jewry's longing for Jerusalem — which now forms one boundary of the Jewish Quarter. The Christian Quarter surrounds the site of Jesus' death and burial, while the small Armenian Quarter harbors a Christian community that has inhabited the same spot for 1,600 years.

The map at left indicates the approximate boundaries of the four quarters, as well as the major religious monuments and important streets. In the maze of lanes and alleys, the churches, synagogues and mosques jostle for space with ordinary dwellings.

In the Muslim Quarter of the Old City, television aerials surmount limestone houses built in a style that has hardly changed over the centuries. Jerusalem's center has probably been inhabited continuously for 4,000 years.

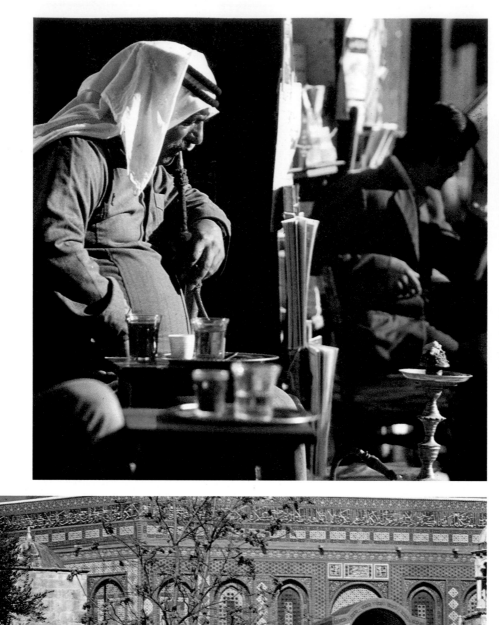

At one of the many cafés in the crowded Muslim Quarter, a customer with a glass of mint tea at his elbow smokes a hookah. Each establishment has its faithful habitués — Arab men who regard the place as a second home.

Men gather for Friday-morning prayers in front of the ornate façade of the Dome of the Rock, the majestic mosque that was built in 691 A.D. and refurbished in the 16th century. It stands on one of Islam's holiest places: the rock from which Muhammad was taken up into heaven.

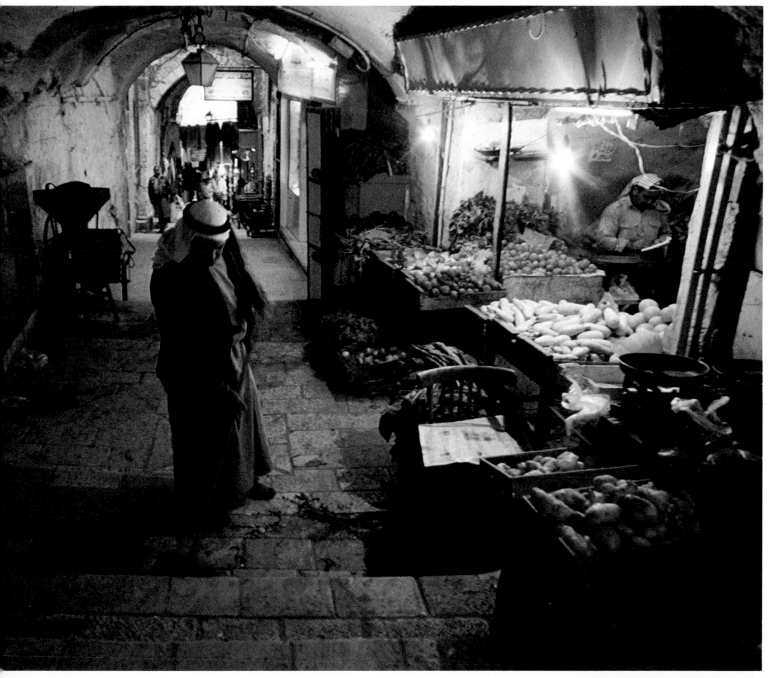

In the medieval covered market in the
Muslim Quarter, where the Old
City's commercial life is concentrated,
a vendor sweeps the pavement in front
of his lamplit vegetable stall. The
Muslim market's busiest time is on Sat-
urday, the Jewish Sabbath, when all the
Jewish shops are shut.

In a square in the Armenian Quarter, members of a family gather outside their house. The quarter — which has some buildings that date back to the time of the Crusades — is a city within a city, enclosed by thick walls. Many of its residents earn their living by making jewelry.

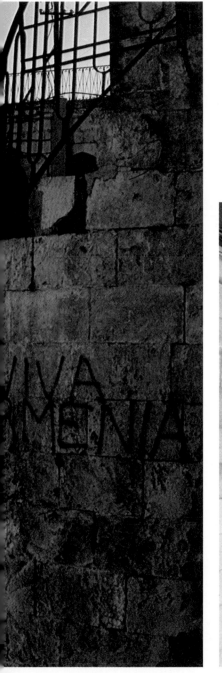

Observed by a cowled monk, a young seminarian at the Armenian cathedral of St. James beats a wooden sounding board. The board, and the metal one beside it, have summoned worshippers to prayer since the 16th century, when Ottoman rulers forbade bell ringing.

Sanitation workers in one of the narrow alleys of the Jewish Quarter *(left)* perch on their vehicle to let a pedestrian edge past. Although the Muslim Quarter is the largest, the Jewish population of the Old City now outnumbers that of the other three quarters.

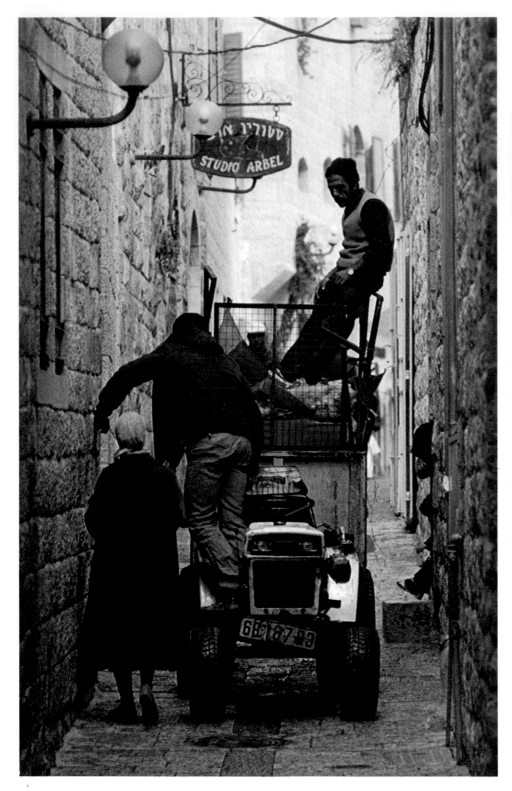

Children dash across the Hurva Square *(right)*, one of the Jewish Quarter's carefully renovated areas. Since 1967, when Israel reclaimed those parts of the city previously held by Jordan, the quarter has been the focus of an ambitious program of rebuilding.

Ethiopian monks sit reading outside their cell-like rooms above the Church of the Holy Sepulcher, the Christian Quarter's holiest shrine. Since the 19th century, when they were banished by rival sects from the building, the Ethiopians have laid claim to the roof.

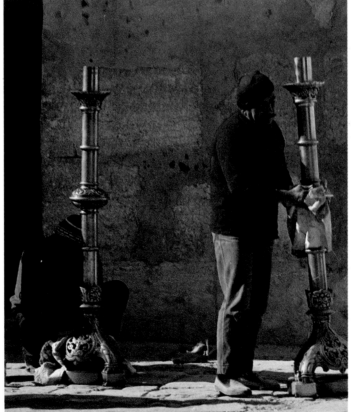

On the sunlit steps of the Holy Sepulcher, two Arab Christians polish a pair of giant candlesticks. Most of the people in the Christian Quarter are of Arab extraction, educated in Christian schools. Since 1948, the Christian population of the Old City has fallen from about 25,000 to 10,000.

THE CHRISTIAN QUARTER

Franciscan monks lead a procession of
pilgrims along the Via Dolorosa —
the Street of Sorrows — the route Jesus
is believed to have followed to Calvary.
Beginning at the Antonia Fortress,
the road passes through the Muslim
Quarter and finishes at the Church of
the Holy Sepulcher.

COEXISTING WITH MINORITIES

A veiled Palestinian Arab woman looks out from her shop in a village near Hebron on the West Bank. About 800,000 Palestinian Arabs live in this territory, which was occupied by Israel in 1967. More than 500,000 other Arabs within Israel's pre-1967 borders are full-fledged citizens of the state.

The Declaration of Independence, issued by Israel's founders on the eve of statehood, proclaimed the right of the Jewish people to national revival in the land that was the birthplace of their faith. Recalling the Diaspora, the early struggles of Zionism and the horrors of the Holocaust, it also set out the ideals upon which the state was to be based. Israel, it asserted, would uphold "the full social and political equality of all its citizens without distinction of religion, race or sex." And it continued, "In the midst of wanton agression, we yet call upon the Arab inhabitants of the State of Israel to preserve the ways of peace and play their part in the development of the State, on the basis of full and equal citizenship."

In its short existence, Israel has had a remarkable record of making some of its ideals work in practice. It has, for example, been conspicuously successful in welding a nation from the disparate elements of its Jewish population. But integrating its Arab inhabitants has proved a much more painful and perplexing problem. Israel has yet to resolve the apparent contradiction of preserving itself as a Jewish homeland while at the same time aspiring to be a secular democracy with equal rights for all its citizens, Jew and Arab alike.

One out of every seven Israeli citizens — some 600,000 out of a total population of 4.3 million — is an Arab. Outside the state's internationally recognized borders, but within the areas occupied since the 1967 war, live nearly 1.4 million other Arabs — 111,000 in the part of Jerusalem formerly held by Jordan, 800,000 outside the city in the territory that Israelis call Judaea and Samaria but the rest of the world knows as the West Bank, and 450,000 in Gaza.

These territories are ruled by a military administration, and their Arab residents do not have Israeli citizenship. Their status and future pose questions that must be resolved in the search for a lasting peace in the Middle East.

Until this peace is achieved, Arab citizens of the state of Israel remain in a difficult position. Whatever their political views, they are, ethnically and religiously, closer kin to their country's enemies than they are to their Jewish fellow citizens. But to generalize about the Arabs is as impossible as it is to do so about the Jews. Culturally, religiously and economically, Israeli Arabs are anything but homogeneous. The prosperous, Westernized Arab businessman or the politically radical university student have more in common with their Jewish-Israeli counterparts than they do with each other. And both feel equally alien to the Bedouin shepherd, dwelling in a carpeted tent.

In religion, the Arab population is surprisingly diverse. About 75 percent are Muslims. Another 14 percent profess Christianity, most as Greek Catholics — affiliated to Rome — or as Greek Orthodox communicants; many are

4

Near Nablus, on the misty summit of
Mount Gerizim, a site sacred to Israel's
550 Samaritans, a priest celebrates
the Samaritan version of the feast of
Passover. Last remnants of a sect that
emerged in the fifth century B.C., they
believe that they alone are the true
spiritual heirs of the 12 tribes of Israel.

descended from Arabs converted by the European missionaries during the Crusades. And defining themselves as neither Christian nor Muslim are 47,000 Druze, members of a self-contained religion that split from Islam in the 11th century. The Druze dogma is jealously guarded, known only to an elite within the tightly knit Druze community, which is scattered throughout the mountainous regions of Syria, Lebanon and northern Israel.

The Druze in Israel have always believed that cooperation with the Jews is in their own best interests; they are the only Israeli Arabs who, at the request of their leaders, do compulsory service in the Israeli Defense Forces; the only exceptions are the 15,000 Druze of the Golan Heights, formerly Syrian subjects, who remained neutral during the fighting with Syria in 1973. Famous for their bravery, many Druze soldiers go on to careers in the frontier police, patrolling the northern borders.

All other Arab citizens are exempted from military service. It would put Israeli Arabs in an impossible moral position, say Israeli authorities, if they were asked to fight against other Arabs from hostile states. The average Israeli Jew does not always appreciate the finer points of this dilemma: "Until they do national service, like we do," flatly declares one Jerusalemite, "they cannot be equal."

Arabs, too, regard this exclusion as an indication of their status as second-class citizens. They may appreciate the freedom from conscription and reserve duty, but they pay a price; anyone who does not serve in the military misses out on the many benefits — grants, scholarships, mortgage assistance and other financial aid — designed to compensate Israeli citizen-soldiers for the time

they lose from their civilian careers.

Throughout the state, the Arabs and the Jews still reside mainly in separate communities. In the countryside, Arab villages lie apart from Jewish settlements; in the cities, Arabs occupy different neighborhoods. There are sizable Arab minorities in Jaffa, Haifa and Acre. Jaffa, once Palestine's principal port and the landing place of centuries of Holy Land pilgrims, has now been absorbed into the larger city of Tel Aviv. Here, an estimated 15,000 Arabs are crowded into the slum streets of the Ajami and Jabalyeh quarters, whose squalor contrasts with the modern, if monotonous, Jewish apartment complexes nearby. Jaffa's Arabs work mostly for small private contractors — Jewish, Christian or Muslim — who hire them, often by the day, for unskilled work in building, street-cleaning, dishwashing or agriculture. Israeli newspapers such as the liberal *Ha'eretz* have campaigned for the Jaffa Arabs to be rehoused, with little result.

In Haifa, the picture is different. This port town, as it climbs up Mount Carmel, has an appearance of great solidity, and its Arab minority includes a number of wealthy merchants and contractors. At rush hours, buses are crowded with Arab workers heading for the industrial area around Haifa Bay and Arab students bound for the university or for Israel's elite scientific institute, the Technion. Above the city, in the Carmel mountains, prosperous farmers and small business owners reside in trim, well-kept Druze villages. Their houses display an unusual preference for windows of all shapes and sizes, often on the same façade.

Farther north, surrounded by palms, lies the walled town of Acre, now a tourist spot. In the older, crowded Arab

CONTRASTING ARAB LIFESTYLES

As is clear from their lifestyles, religions and political attitudes, Israeli Arabs are far from being a homogeneous community. The Druze, for example, who belong to a secret religion that broke away from Islam in the 11th century, have become thoroughly integrated. But many Muslim Palestinians oppose Israeli rule, and their coreligionists, the Bedouin, cling to a way of life that has little to do with modern political exigencies.

Yet these groups share cultural traits. Their homes, for example — be they tents or concrete villas — are furnished in a similiar style, and the women withdraw when male guests arrive.

Wearing the hat and scarf that mark him as an initiate in the mysteries of his sect, a Druze elder *(right)* stands at his door. His "welcoming room" *(below)* has Western-style furniture in addition to a variety of rugs and colorful cushions for Arab visitors.

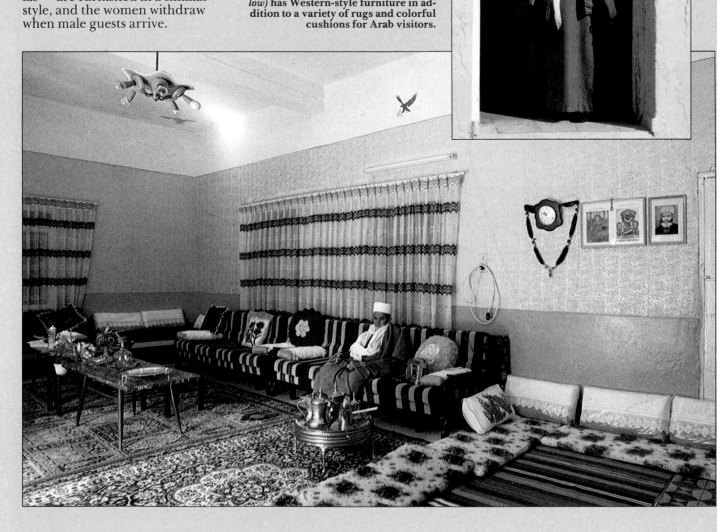

In the living room of their three-room house *(below)*, a Palestinian youth drinks mint tea with his father. Behind them, pictures of Arab entertainers share space with typical Palestinian embroidery and a rug depicting Mecca.

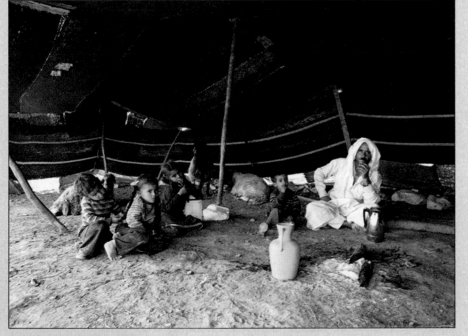

Accompanied by his children and some of his sheep, a Bedouin enjoys a glass of tea in his woven goat-hair tent. Most Bedouin tents are divided into two parts: Women retire to their own area to cook or when guests appear.

part of the town, robed Muslim dignitaries walk silently to prayers through the courtyard of the domed Al-Jazzar mosque with its slender minarets; it sometimes seems that little has changed since the Ottomans ruled.

To the west of Haifa, in the lush vale of Jezreel, some Israeli kibbutzim have established high-tech industrial enterprises. To the regret of the kibbutz movement's traditionalists, hired Arabs have taken the place of the collectives' own members in the fields.

In Galilee, beyond Nazareth, Muslim and Druze farming villages lie between Jewish settlements. The ancient villages seem to have grown out of the stony landscape, but the flourishing crops in the fields around them indicate that Arab farmers, like their Jewish neighbors, are reaping the benefits of modern farming methods and better equipment. Quietly prosperous, the local Arab population has now outstripped the Jewish population, and Arabs once again — as they did before statehood — form the majority in Galilee.

In the coastal plain between Haifa and Hadera lies the so-called Arab triangle, a tight nucleus of villages where the farmers, like their counterparts in Galilee, have moved from subsistence farming to the more intensive cultivation of cash crops. The visible signs of this progress often disappoint the tourist photographers, who prefer their Arab villagers in unchanging biblical poses — barefoot *fellahin* painfully dragging plows over rocky soil, shepherds with their pipes and goats, women carrying water jars to the well. Nevertheless, the villages in the triangle have prospered and expanded, sharing to some extent the economic growth of Israel as a whole. Farming is no longer the only source of income. Here, as in

107

other parts of the country, Arabs have replaced Jewish workers on building sites and now dominate the construction industry, not only as unskilled laborers but as supervisors and prosperous independent contractors.

To find the more exotic Arab of their fantasies, sight-seers are compelled to travel south into the Negev, home to about 40,000 Bedouin. Yet even these desert nomads are slowly being settled in permanent sites. For some years, the authorities unsuccessfully tried to persuade the Bedouin to move into modern high-density housing. Eventually realizing that many of them strongly preferred their traditional tents, the government changed its policy. Now extended-family groups are given vacant plots for development. Some still live in tents, others in shacks, a few in large villas. Many families have modern houses — which they use, mainly as storerooms, continuing to eat and sleep in tents pitched alongside.

Less interested than other Arabs in the politics of the world outside, these Bedouin instead focus their attentions on the weekly market in Beersheba, where, as of old, they haggle energetically over sheep, chickens, herbs, spices and traditional handicrafts, as well as more prosaic manufactured goods. The vendors of intricate Bedouin bracelets and those of bright plastic buckets ply their wares side by side with no sense of incongruity.

The Israeli authorities are eager to note the qualitative improvement in the lives not only of the Bedouin but of all Israeli Arabs since 1948. Before then, few if any Arab villages had running water or electricity; by 1972 the national electricity grid had reached nearly every Arab village, and there was running water in every house. Arabs, like all Israelis, enjoy far better health today than before independence; life expectancy has increased from 54 in 1948 to over 70 in the 1980s. They are also better educated: By 1984, 95 percent of Arab-Israeli children were enrolled in school, and more than 2,000 Arab students attended Israeli universities, while another 1,000 studied abroad.

But for the Arabs of Israel, an improvement in living conditions is not the only point at issue. There are other, and deeper, forces in the Arab-Jew equation: forces of hatred, fear and pride that have distorted the relationship of the two peoples, despite their common ancestry and religious roots.

In response to the growth of Zionism at the end of the 19th century, a new nationalist consciousness emerged in Palestine. Many of its first activists came from the small, highly educated elite of wealthy landowning families in Jerusalem. (Ironically, others of the same group were profitably selling out to Zionist buyers.) But political literacy was not solely the preserve of the rich: Teachers, shopkeepers and government clerks, who now served the British as they had served the Ottomans before them, were aware of nationalist stirrings elsewhere in the Arab world.

The Zionist settlers and their alien ways troubled this Muslim society. For centuries, the Arabs of Palestine had tolerated small, impoverished communities of pious Jews who had lived quietly among themselves. But these brash newcomers — with their irreligious socialism, their barelegged women working in the fields with the men — offended Arab sensibilities.

The turbulence of the years that followed drove the two peoples even further apart. The hope of early Zionists that the Jew and Arab might share the efforts and rewards of building a new Palestine together became an ever more unlikely fantasy. As Zionist activity increased, Arab militancy grew. When the British appointed the young Arab nationalist Amin al Husseini (member of one of Palestine's largest landowning families) as mufti of Jerusalem in 1921, the pattern for the next three decades was set.

The red-bearded Husseini, universally acknowledged as a "charmer" and a "suave diplomat," leading a coalition of Palestinian clan leaders, urban professionals and rising political activists, was implacable in his opposition to Zionism. He refused to accept the presence of the Zionists in Palestine or to negotiate with them directly on any issue. But while the Arab nationalists declined to yield at all, the Zionists took a more pragmatic course, purchasing a little more land in one place, building a Jewish school or hospital in another — keeping pace with international opinion and confident of the ultimate triumph of Jewish nationalism.

Ironically, the mufti gave his support to the Nazis in Germany, whose persecution of Jews was ultimately what created an international consensus in favor of the Jewish state. Husseini's propaganda broadcasts during the war, sponsored by the Nazi government, landed him in a French prison on a charge of collaboration.

In the Jordan River in Galilee, a Pentecostal minister and his helper baptize a swimsuited woman while others wait their turn. Many of Israel's 96,000 Christians and thousands of foreign pilgrims choose to be baptized in the river — as Christ was 2,000 years ago.

After the new Jewish state had declared its independence and defeated its Arab opponents in the bloody conflict that followed, the Arabs named the events of 1947 to 1949 "the Great Disaster." By the time the fighting ended, an indeterminate number of Arabs — possibly half a million people — had fled the new state of Israel, leaving behind about 167,000 Arabs, mostly poor peasants. Some families had managed to leave with most of their possessions before the fighting started and had resettled themselves in newly thriving Arab states, such as Kuwait; others found homes farther away, in Europe or the Americas. But the majority of the Arab refugees, less fortunate, spent a wretched winter huddled in Gaza or in Jordan, Syria or Lebanon. It was the Palestine Arabs who were now scattered, in their own diaspora.

The homeless Palestinians, many of them women and children, were gathered into 53 United Nations Relief Works Agency (UNRWA) camps in Jordan, Syria, Lebanon and Gaza, which the Egyptians had annexed at the end of the war. The camps were a breeding ground for a rising nationalist group called the Palestine National Liberation Movement, later absorbed by the Palestine Liberation Organization. Its members expressed the frustrations of their people, despairing of any help from their host countries, which had

A YOUNG RELIGION WITH A FAITH IN HUMAN UNITY

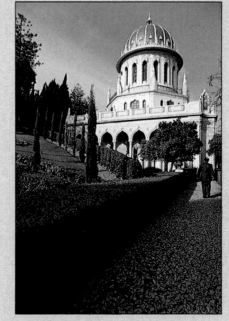

The Baha'i shrine in Haifa.

Israel is the world center of Bahaism, a faith inspired by the teachings of Mirza Ali Mohammed, a 19th-century Persian mystic. After he was martyred in 1850, his doctrine was expanded by disciple and compatriot Baha' Allah (Splendor of God). The religion combines elements of Islam, Christianity and Judaism and teaches the essential unity of mankind.

Only a handful of the hundreds of thousands of Bahais live in Israel; the rest are scattered worldwide. But the faith found its base here when Baha' Allah, after years of wandering, ended his days in Palestine. In 1899, seven years after Baha' Allah's death, followers had Mirza Ali Mohammed's body brought to Haifa and entombed in a shrine, which was later topped with a golden dome — a gift from believers around the world.

109

4

resolutely kept them in their camps. By 1959, one of its leaders, Yasser Arafat, was preaching that the Palestinians should rely only on themselves for the liberation of their country and that their weapons would be terrorism and guerrilla warfare.

At first, life was not much easier for the Arabs who remained in Israel after 1948. Most of the main concentra-tions of Arab settlement fell within the "security zones" in the border regions, which were under military rule. Here, lands were confiscated, whole villages were razed and their inhabitants reset-tled. Villagers who wanted to travel outside their own districts had to have permits from military authorities; cur-fews were imposed and communica-tions often suspended. Arabs felt that the government often invoked "securi-ty reasons" to justify their oppression of the non-Jewish population. Not until 1966 were the military restrictions lift-ed, the application of regulations liber-alized, and Arab workers allowed to join the Israeli General Federation of Labor, the Histadrut.

Despite these reforms, many Israeli Arabs still question Israel's assertion that it accords full equal rights to all its citizens. Although public notices are bi-

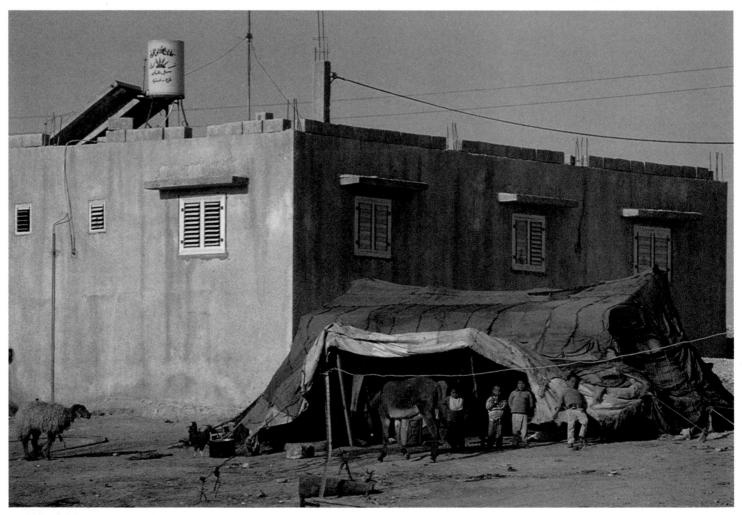

Bedouin children stand outside a tent pitched in front of their house near Beersheba. The government has con-structed houses for many of the nomads to encourage them to settle, but this building is used mostly as a storeroom — and the family continues to live in its traditional dwelling.

lingual, and although Islam, like Judaism and Christianity, is a recognized religion, Arab-Israelis often feel the victims of discrimination.

Although Arab citizens enjoy the same voting rights as other Israelis, many of them resent the fact that there is no specifically Arab political party. The government, giving the official excuse of "national security," refuses to permit the formation of any political grouping that might espouse the cause of Arab nationalism. Arab towns and villages have their own democratically elected local councils, filled from a slate of Arab candidates; and in general elections, Israel's political parties compete hard for Arab votes. Among the 120 members of the Knesset, there are usually between seven and 10 Arab members, most of whom are from the centrist and left-wing parties. The long-established Communist party, for example — officially anti-Zionist though not against the state of Israel's existence — has traditionally been a natural magnet for the Arab protest vote.

Despite official Israeli statistics that show continuous progress for Israeli Arabs in education, housing, health and purchasing power, the Arabs unsurprisingly compare the quality of their lives with the even higher standards of their Jewish neighbors. The Israeli statistics do not reveal that there are upper limits to Arab progress, but according to a 1984 United States State Department report on human rights, fewer than 2 percent of Israel's senior government officials and 3 percent of judges were Arabs, although Arabs made up 15 percent of the country's population. No large bank or industrial enterprise was headed by an Arab; and in Israeli universities, only 3 percent of students and an even smaller percent-

age of the members of the academic staff were Arabs.

The usual Israeli reply to criticisms such as these is that as long as the wider Arab-Israeli conflict continues unabated, it is unlikely that Arabs will be appointed to senior government or civil service posts, except in special cases. Ambitious Arab graduates are faced with few options: the so-called free professions, such as medicine, law, engineering, teaching and journalism. And even in these fields, Arabs feel there are limits to their advancement.

Discrimination operates, according to the Arabs, throughout the economic spectrum. They claim that many Arab farmers, whose lands were confiscated, have been reduced to day laborers on Jewish cooperative farms and kibbutzim. In industry, Arabs feel they are left with the low-paid, unskilled jobs, while Jewish workers move into the better-paid areas of high technology and defense-related industries.

Polarization, however, begins long before people enter the work force. Jewish children automatically go to Hebrew-language state schools, and Arab children go to parallel Arabic-

language state schools. Only when they reach higher education do the two groups converge. Even then, many young Arabs resent the fact that they must pass the *Bagrut* examination in Jewish history and literature before they can go on to the university level. Not surprisingly, Arabs who are fortunate enough to enter the universities often feel themselves in an alien environment. Their Arab student unions are given official blessing but remain a guarded refuge, where memories of the Great Disaster mingle uneasily with frustration, militancy and an unquenchable national pride.

At the University of Haifa, where Arabs make up 10 percent of the student body, a special Arab-Jewish center has been set up to promote coexistence and "shatter mutually hostile stereotyping." The center awards scholarships to Arab students and arranges preacademic courses for them in Hebrew and English. Arab students cooperate in research into Arab life in Israel and the Middle East as a whole. In Middle East studies, both Jewish and Arab lecturers have been appointed, in an effort to present a balanced picture. Yet even

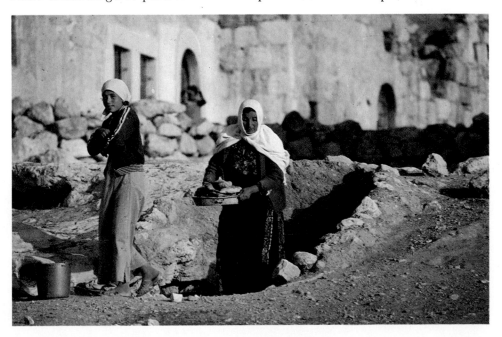

Carrying the day's bread, a Palestinian woman and her daughter emerge from their centuries-old underground oven. The bread is leavened with a starter, fermented dough from a previous batch, and is baked on hot stones — a method used for at least 12,000 years.

4

the most enthusiastic supporters accept that a liberal academic island of coexistence in a place like Haifa Unversity will remain just that — an island — so long as the general Arab-Israeli conflict remains unresolved.

Suspicion, contempt or outright dislike between members of different ethnic groups is not unique to Israel, but the unresolved hostilities between the Jewish state and the Arab world do nothing to help the problems of prejudice at home. Many Arabs feel they are victims of negative attitudes that range from mild distrust to sheer bigotry.

Although cases of Israeli Arabs harming their Jewish compatriots are extremely rare, Arabs complain that the Jews can never rid themselves of the notion that the Israeli Arabs constitute a fifth column within their boundaries. In the 1970s, the many incursions by guerrillas of the Palestine Liberation Organization did nothing to alleviate such fears. Between 1977 and 1984, tensions between Arabs and Jews increased even more under the rightwing Likud government. Arabs saw a sharp swing toward a new assertive Jewish nationalism: The Gush Emunim, an extremist group composed largely of North American immigrants, claimed the West Bank to be Jewish by divine right, as part of the Biblical land of Israel. In 1985, a group of Jewish terrorists were convicted of the murder of three Palestinian students in Hebron, a town on the West Bank; other members of the same organization were accused of conspiring to blow up the Dome of the Rock, the sacred Muslim site on the Temple mount in Jerusalem. Not surprisingly, many Israeli Arabs — particularly among the student population — sympathized with the anti-Israel views of the PLO.

Young Arabs walk to their school near Mount Carmel. Education is compulsory for all children in Israel, including those in the occupied areas. Arabs are taught their own language and culture, but after the age of nine they are also required to learn Hebrew.

Yet even in the midst of conflict, some attempts are being made to heal the rifts and smash the myths that engender prejudice. A new coexistence course, entitled "The Arab Citizens of Israel" is now a feature of the curriculum of Jewish-Israeli schools, and an equivalent program has been introduced into the Arabic-language system. For many young Jews and Arabs, the course provides a unique opportunity to meet their counterparts face to face; they do not flinch from asking hard questions and telling difficult truths.

"Why," asked one Jewish student, "should I accept someone like you, who gives legitimacy to the PLO? They want to kill me."

"I believe that the PLO is the representative of the Palestinian people. Okay, I am part of the Palestinian people . . . but I see myself as a citizen of Israel, entitled to equal rights."

In the zones occupied by Israel after the Six Day War of 1967, Arabs today still live under military restrictions, as Israeli Arabs did until 1966. Many consider themselves in a political limbo while the international community de-

112

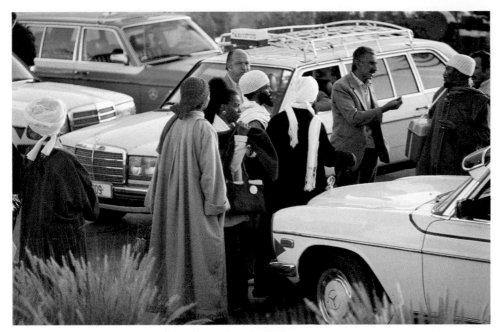

bates their future. Recent history has placed the Jerusalem Arabs in a particularly difficult position, victims of the intense nationalist and religious passions that both Jew and Arab feel for the city. Yet for the most part the two peoples coexist harmoniously. Ethnic tensions erupt here far less often than they do in other areas with polarized populations; the atmosphere in Jerusalem is infinitely more tranquil than, for instance, in Belfast.

The Arab name for Jerusalem is *al-Quds al-Sharif*, which means "the Holy and Noble City." Here, in the Seventh century A.D., the Arabs built a mosque, the Dome of the Rock, to mark the spot where Muhammad himself is said to have departed on his journey to heaven. The Jews' attachment to the city is equally powerful, going back nearly 3,000 years. The Psalms praised the ancient capital as a "perfection of beauty"; the prophet Isaiah called it "the faithful city full of justice, in which righteousness lodged."

To Jews, the recovery of Jerusalem was a homecoming of deep emotional significance; to Arabs, it seemed only to emphasize the humiliation they suf-

fered in the Great Disaster; they had their doubts about Isaiah's encomium to Jewish justice and righteousness. When Israel annexed the previously Jordanian half of the city and declared Jerusalem the capital, the United Nations refused to recognize the annexation; many foreign governments kept their embassies in the former capital, Tel Aviv. Encouraged by these gestures, many Arabs retained a hope that they might, in the future, become masters of their own destiny in Jerusalem.

In the aftermath of the Six Day War, the task of reuniting the fragmented city fell to its new Jewish mayor, Teddy Kollek. He took it upon himself to oppose what he saw as the bias of the government and its tendency to ignore the needs of Jerusalem's Arabs. He objected to policies that would transform Greater Jerusalem into a purely Jewish capital, guarded by strategically placed Jewish suburbs along the skyline. Jerusalem, he insisted, should be a city with an international flavor, where Jews and Arabs respected each other as fellow citizens. Through mortgage companies linked to the municipality, he conjured up thousands of loans for Arabs want-

ing to build their own homes, and he saw to it that Arabs received their share of new school buildings and recreational facilities. Above all, he demanded that Arabs be employed at every level of local government. In return, Arabs turned out in large numbers to vote for Kollek in municipal elections, ignoring PLO calls for them to boycott the polls.

Kollek's pragmatic politics seemed to provide the only solution to the anomalies that confronted the Israelis when they first annexed East Jerusalem. They discovered, for example, that in legal terms Jerusalem's Arabs became Israeli inhabitants while remaining Jordanian citizens; they thus acquired the problematic status of resident enemy aliens. The Israelis found it difficult to persuade Arab professionals, owners of businesses or company directors to apply for licenses under Israeli law, to pay Israeli taxes, or to conform with laws applying to the employment of municipal workers.

Some laws, the Israeli authorities decided, were best left unenforced; the others have been amended to make special provisions for the Jerusalem Arabs, who are now entitled — but not compelled — to become Israeli citizens. The Muslim religious courts, which operate in accordance with the Islamic laws of Jordan, have been left intact, and Muslim control over the Temple mount retained. An attempt to impose an Israeli curriculum in the Arabic-language East Jerusalem schools resulted in demonstrations by pupils and teachers, and most Arab parents simply transferred their children to private schools that followed a Jordanian curriculum. Eventually, the authorities quietly dropped the issue.

For many Jerusalem Arabs, Israeli annexation has made little difference

In a marble factory on the West Bank, a Palestinian cuts stone for export to Jordan. Israelis point out that the economies of the occupied territories have improved since 1967, and unemployment among the Arabs is now only slightly more than 1 percent.

to their way of life: In some respects they are better off economically than they were before. After the Israelis restored and rebuilt parts of the city, tourism increased, and the Arab quarter — chaotic, crowded and noisy — has lost none of its character. Chic Arab-owned boutiques and shops cater to the foreigners thronging the cobbled alleys to haggle for carpets, brassware and "antiquities" of dubious age. Middle-class Arabs have become more prosperous, and they patronize the same international hotels and restaurants as Jews. On Saturdays, when Jewish shops are closed for the Sabbath, long lines of cars bring Jewish customers eager to stock up on provisions at the Arab shops in the Old City, which is now inhabited almost exclusively by the middle classes. Many of the wealthier Arabs have moved into the suburbs of Greater Jerusalem to live in more spacious surroundings.

Jerusalem has long had a substantial population of Arab professional people; many of the older generation received a European education under the British mandate. The city is still provided with power by the Arab-run Jerusalem Electricity Company and serviced by Arab doctors, lawyers and municipal officials working alongside Jewish colleagues. Many members of the Knesset, Jews as well as Arabs, have Arab secretaries. Arab journalists staff the four Arab newspapers published in Jerusalem and produce the programs for Israel's Arab radio and the Arabic-language television.

Despite a climate of prosperity and productivity, Jerusalem Arabs are still not reconciled to Israeli annexation. The warp of bitter Arab antagonism toward Zionism is now woven with a weft of fatalistic resignation to the ap-

parent permanence of the Israeli presence. Many Jerusalem Arabs regard the PLO, once their best hope of self-determination, as a spent force. They have seen new Israeli settlements, which were heavily subsidized and encouraged by previous governments, surround the city on former Arab land, and they have watched the Jewish population of Jerusalem rise to become the majority. They feel oppressed by the Israeli censorship of Arab newspapers, which has often been crudely exercised in the name of "security." They draw little comfort from the freedom of expression — which frequently espouses Arab causes — that is enjoyed by the Jewish press, only noting that the official censorship regulations seldom seem to be applied with equal rigor to Hebrew-language newspapers.

The atmosphere is perceptibly different outside Jerusalem, in the 2,125

square miles of the West Bank proper. Although only the fringes of the Arab population actively resisted the Israeli occupation, resentment remains widespread. But the Arabs themselves have yet to agree on a desirable alternative. Some are supporters of the PLO; others are less keen on the domination of what they see as a faction-ridden movement. Older Palestinians have unpleasant memories of the years of harsh Jordanian rule between 1949 and 1967, and there is no desire for close links with undemocratic Syria. Faced with such a Hobson's choice, few West Bank Arabs could foresee any prospect of genuinely democratic self-rule that would accommodate peaceful coexistence with their Israeli neighbor.

North of Jerusalem in the West Bank lies Nablus, a quiet town of villas and small gardens. A center of Arab nationalism, with a new Jewish settlement on

An Arab baker in Hebron displays a platter of *baklava* — pastry layered with nuts and honey. In Israel, both Jews and Arabs have a passion for these desserts, which are thought to have originated in ancient Persia.

the skyline and an Arab university below, it is the site of a large refugee camp. Nablus is also the home of noted writer Raymonda Tawil, one of a number of Palestinian intellectuals who have kept alight the flame of nationalism. In her book *My Home My Prison* (first published in Tel Aviv), Tawil relates how in 1967, on the second day of the Six Day War, she and her friends saw a column of tanks rumbling down the main street. At first she imagined them to be a unit from a friendly Arab army — Algerians, perhaps, or Iraqis — come to help the Palestinians in their hour of need. And then she realized, to her horror, that these were Israeli troops: After barely two days of fight-

ing, they had driven the Jordanians from the West Bank and the Egyptians from the Gaza Strip. This moment, she admits, shattered any illusion that Israel might be defeated or might somehow cease to exist.

Neither Gaza nor the West Bank had been treated well by its previous rulers. Gaza, a small citrus-growing center and Mediterranean fishing port, had in 1948 been overrun by Palestinian refugees. They were accommodated in UNRWA camps, hastily built townships with monotonous rows of minimal houses. Relief workers doled out adequate food rations and clothing and provided good schools and medical service, but there were few other amen-

ities; life in the camps was bearable, but bleak. Yet, apart from receiving a few hundred Gaza students into Egyptian universities, the Egyptian government, which had sovereignty over the area, did little for the Gaza refugees. They were simply kept on site, bored, depressed and resentful.

On the larger, Jordanian-held West Bank, the 1948 refugees constituted a much smaller proportion of the Arab population. Indeed, if work had become available, they might well have been absorbed into the community. The Jordanian government, however, playing safe, concentrated all of its economic development and interest on the opposite side of the Jordan river. And

Jordanian rule was not gentle, as the Palestinian refugees rapidly discovered. Jordan allowed them no freedom of speech, denied them a free press and refused to permit any autonomous political organization. All political parties on the West Bank were abolished; Jordan's military intelligence force was active everywhere.

After their stunning victory in the Six Day War, the Israelis had apparently intended to return the whole of Sinai to Egypt and the Golan Heights to Syria, in exchange for guarantees of peace and demilitarization. They had also hoped to negotiate an agreement over the West Bank with King Hussein of Jordan. But an Arab summit conference in Khartoum that year rejected compromise in what came to be called the "triple no": no peace with Israel, no recognition, no negotiation.

In the ensuing deadlock, the Israelis found themselves with tempting land on their doorstep. First into the territories had been the Israeli military and administrators; now came businesses seeking trade and employers seeking Arab workers. Later came religious militants of the Gush Emunim.

The Israeli government resolved that the territories had to be pacified. In the Gaza camps the PLO had left guerrillas behind, and Arabs accused of cooperating with Israel were assassinated. The Israelis set themselves to root out active resistance — and succeeded. They did the same on the West Bank, where the Jordanians had, in 1967, conveniently left behind intelligence files on West Bank militants.

In September 1970, King Hussein decided that the PLO posed an increasing threat to the security of Jordan and moved to expel it from his country. After a period of heavy fighting, known later by the PLO as Black September, Hussein succeeded. Once the threat of guerrilla raids from Jordan was removed, Moshe Dayan — then Israeli minister of defense — declared that the bridges across the Jordan should be thrown open. Within a year, an estimated 100,000 Arab visitors came across the bridges to the West Bank and Israel, and West Bank farmers and businesses traded freely with the Jordanians as well as the Israelis.

The Yom Kippur War of 1973, however, again threw a shadow over the West Bank. In the following year, King Hussein of Jordan, despite his earlier opposition, acknowledged the PLO as the sole representative of the Palestinian people; many West Bank residents welcomed the move with enthusiasm. The Israelis tried to counter this Arab nationalist upsurge by stricter rule, exiling two pro-PLO Arab mayors, dismissing others and creating a conservative Arab Village League to oppose PLO activity. A tense situation was made worse when extremist Jewish settlers entered the fray as counterterrorists, badly injuring the mayors of two Arab communities.

The Likud government of 1977 to 1984 was accused by its opponents of having violated the concept of "local and cultural autonomy" for the Arabs of the West Bank and Gaza enshrined in the 1979 Camp David agreement between Egypt and Israel. Instead, it effected de facto annexation. Israel faced a crucial dilemma: It could either withhold legal Israeli citizenship from the Arabs of the West Bank and Gaza, or not. If it chose the first option, Israel would no longer be a true democracy, and if the second, the Jewish homeland would become a binational state with two million Arab citizens.

The government made its choice by doing nothing. And so, in the 1980s, two phenomena began to transform the West Bank. First, in spite of objections at home and abroad, the settlement of Israelis in what they called Samaria and Judaea was given the highest priority and proceeded apace. Strategic roads were built, mostly by Arab workers, along with residential settlements and industrial townships. Within two or three years, subsidized cheap housing had transformed parts of the West Bank into an Israeli commuterland. Ordinary Israelis, interviewed in the press, admitted they no longer quite knew where the West Bank ended and where Israel proper began.

Despite these upheavals, Israeli rule has brought material benefits. Statistics show that the people of the West Bank and Gaza have made steady progress in education, enjoy improved hospital facilities and better health, and possess more consumer goods. More than 60,000 Arab workers commute to work in Israeli industries and agriculture in places such as Beersheba and Ashdod, close to the occupied zones.

The other agent of change has been the presence of five Arab university institutions that now serve the West Bank and Gaza, where there had been none before. The presence of between 11,000 and 12,000 Arab students has produced a marked social change in the occupied areas. As a new educated class, they have embraced the Palestinian cause. At Bir Zeit University on the West Bank, students have supported the PLO by strikes, demonstrations, road blocks and occasionally by throwing stones at Israeli traffic. The Israelis have responded angrily to these provocations with temporary shutdowns, political censorship and,

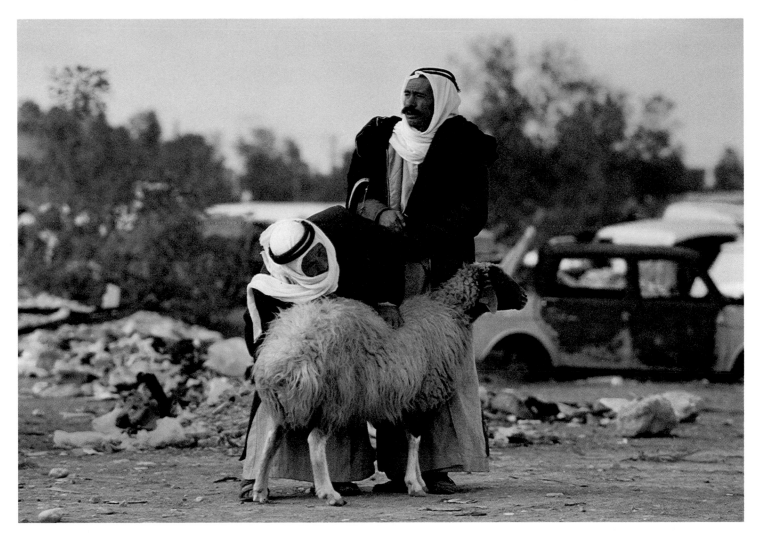

when riots have erupted, with shooting.

Although the status of Arabs living in the occupied zones remains unresolved, there have been signs of an easing of tensions. The government has lifted some of the most galling restrictions on West Bank Arabs. In the United States, a consortium of some of the wealthiest and most influential American Jews and Arabs has established a development bank on the West Bank, and initiated other projects to improve life for the Palestinians.

Such beginnings may bring hope, but no Israeli government can afford to underestimate the dangers. Within the state's official borders and occupied territories live 3.5 million Jews and two million Arabs. And this Arab population itself embraces a world of differences: between noncitizens and citizens, between Muslims and Christians, between the Arab students at Haifa in dialogue with Israeli academics and the Arab students at Bir Zeit University throwing stones in support of the PLO; between the Arab journalists smoothly running Arabic hours on Israeli television and the Arab journalists on the West Bank daily expressing their dislike of Israel; between the conservative ultraorthodox Muslims of Hebron, single-minded in their opposition to Judaism, and the more flexible Christian Arabs of Nazareth, voting Communist.

Given these disparate and conflicting elements, what hope is there for coexistence? The answer may belong to Abu Haled, another Arab writer who, like Ramonda Tawil, saw the Israeli tanks rolling into Nablus in 1967. "Do you know what the hardest thing was for me to swallow?" he asked Israeli journalist Amos Oz. "We are two similar peoples, our fate is interlocked. Am I happy about it? No, not at all. You are not happy about it either. . . . You are our destiny. We are your destiny. . . . There is nothing we can do about it: Here in this land we are welded together, Jews and Arabs, forever." □

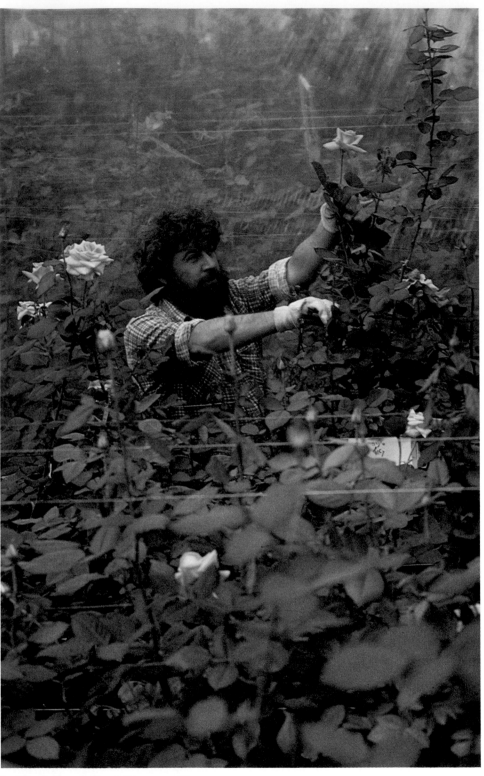

Inside a hothouse devoted to rose cultivation, an Israeli horticulturist prunes blooms that are past their prime. The country began selling cut flowers abroad in the early 1960s, and by 1982, it was Europe's largest supplier.

SEEKING SELF-SUFFICIENCY

"Israel," observed the nation's first president, Chaim Weizmann, "is the only country where miracles are part of state planning."

In a land whose ancient history is one long chronicle of prodigies and wonders, it is hardly surprising that the economic growth of the modern state should be hailed as miraculous. By any standard, Israel's material progress—the speed of its development over a few strife-torn decades—has been remarkable. In the years since independence, despite dislocations caused by war, shortages of food and raw materials, and an economy that has sometimes teetered on the brink of collapse, Israel has transformed itself from a struggling, essentially agrarian state into a Westernized, high-technology society.

But the story of Israel's dramatic economic growth, and its equally dramatic economic crises, is less a saga of divine intervention than a tale of human pragmatism amid the hard political facts of 20th-century life. It is also a story that starts generations before its official beginning.

The Jewish community began to lay the foundations for statehood at least 50 years before it had a land. And the nation's founders had a clear idea of what they wanted to create. Reality, however, fell far short of the dream.

Never were a people more ill equipped to colonize a barren country than the Jewish pioneers who came to Palestine between the 1880s and the 1920s. They were filled with Zionist idealism and mostly with a socialist ideology, and they were consumed with a burning desire to rebuild the homeland of Israel. But they knew virtually nothing of cultivation, of draining malaria-ridden swamps, or of creating new industries; and they lacked all the crucial elements of labor, money and technology. And they had no experience in dealing with the Arabs in Palestine. It all had to be learned the hard way.

When the first Zionist immigrants arrived in Palestine in the 1880s, they found a poor, pastoral land, a denuded wilderness of sun, sand and salt. It had only one small river, the Jordan, and streams that dried up in summer. There was no coal, no oil. No precious stones or ores sparkled in the rocky hills or marshy valleys of a place lovingly described in the Bible as "flowing with milk and honey."

Some daunted and disillusioned newcomers went home again, unwilling to face the hardships. But others stayed, determined to change things. The pioneers considered their few assets, decided what they had to do and set about doing it.

"Our people," wrote one of the early Zionist leaders, A. D. Gordon, "can be rejuvenated only if each one of us re-creates himself through labor and life close to nature." But to achieve this, the immigrants needed land.

Sympathetic philanthropists, such as the Baron Edmond de Rothschild, contributed funds. One of the baron's early projects—a winery, established in 1882—provided early immigrants with their first industrial enterprise.

In 1901, the Zionist movement set up the Jewish National Fund as "the eternal possession of the Jewish people." To raise money, the fund placed blue tin collection boxes in Jewish homes throughout the Western world. From the alleys of London's Whitechapel to the slum tenements of New York's Lower East Side, the boxes stood as household symbols of the Jews' longing for a home of their own.

Acreage bought by the fund from Arab and absentee Ottoman landowners was leased to prospective farmers but was not sold in perpetuity. In this, the fund followed the Biblical commandment: "The land shall not be sold for ever and the land is Mine." Even today, land acquired from the Israel Land Authority, which controls most of the agricultural property of the modern-day state, cannot be leased for more than 49 years.

As well as purchasing farmland already in use, the fund devoted its resources to land reclamation and development. It opened up large areas of wasteland to cultivation: the broad Jezreel Valley, for example, which later became one of Israel's main breadbaskets, as well as the loess-covered wilderness of the Negev, stretching over more than half the country.

The fund also used its revenues to reforest the mountains of Palestine, stripped bare by centuries of grazing by goats and sheep. When the early settlers arrived, they noted that the country had few birds, presumably because of the scarcity of trees. The call went out to world Jewry to "plant a tree in Palestine," and succeeding generations have had their births, bar and bath mitzvahs and weddings commemorated by pine, cypress, eucalyptus and carob trees set down in the soil of Israel. Since the early 1900s, the fund has planted more than 100 million of these and other species.

The little blue tin boxes of the Jewish National Fund made a significant contribution to these achievements, but the Zionists needed financing on a larger scale to enable more Jews to settle and work in Palestine. At first, the world banking establishment had not looked kindly on the Zionist cause, and the movement concluded that a banking company of its own was the only solution. In 1899, Zionist leader Theodor Herzl wrote in his diary, "The bank is now our greatest concern. Should we succeed, no one will ever imagine what we had to go through; how much courage it took, for in truth we are boycotted by all the large banking concerns."

In 1902, a year after the establishment of the Jewish National Fund, the World Zionist Organization succeeded in creating the Anglo-Palestine Colonial Trust. By the time of independence in 1948, it had become Palestine's principal financial institution and was funding new factories, farms and business enterprises started up by Jewish immigrants.

At the outbreak of World War II, these farms and factories became a linchpin of British defense in the Middle East. Mobilized by the war effort, Palestinian Jews vastly increased the amount of land under cultivation and built hundreds of new factories to supply the Allies with essential military, technical and medical supplies. By 1943, nearly two thirds of the Jewish work force was employed in defense-related occupations. In the short term, this surge of activity assisted the struggle against the Axis powers; in the long term, it has provided fertile soil for the germination of Israel's economy after independence was achieved.

But when the British walked out on the 14th of May, 1948, after 30 years as the ruling power, they bequeathed a legacy of administrative chaos that had economic repercussions.

Reluctant to give any support to the new nation, the British government froze all sterling assets held in Britain by the former government of Palestine, leaving the fledgling state without foreign currency to import food and other essentials. Israel was forced to borrow, in some cases from unconventional sources. The first finance minister, Eliezer Kaplan, appealed for loans from American Zionists to buy food.

Despite the infrastructure of roads, bridges, airfields and harbors that the British had left behind them, the communications and transportation systems were beset by difficulties. In the beginning, the International Postal Union refused to carry mail originating in Israel. Because of the exorbitant insurance rates imposed by the British-controlled Shipping Conference, a virtual shipping blockade ensued.

Rationing had to be instituted. A black market flourished and prices skyrocketed. As was the case in postwar Europe, the citizens of the new state breakfasted on powdered eggs and drank chicory instead of coffee. Children were allowed to have two fresh eggs a week. Butter was available, but only on a doctor's prescription.

Food was not the only thing in short supply. In 1945, the Arab nations launched a boycott against Zionist enterprises, which, after independence, became a full-scale economic blockade. They threatened to embargo any company that did business with the Jewish state, and they blacklisted those who had invested in Israeli enterprises, joined in partnership with Israeli firms or shipped goods to Israeli ports.

The most serious threat came from the maritime blockade: All Israeli shipping was barred from the Suez Canal, as were vessels of other nations carrying cargo to ports in Israel. In 1949 and 1956, Egypt also blockaded the Strait of Tirān, the only access to the Israeli port of Eilat.

As a result, Israel could not do business with natural trading partners — its nearest neighbors — and, instead, had to import even the most basic commodities from markets hundreds, even thousands, of miles away. Newsprint, for instance, was so hard to come by that newspapers were restricted to two-page editions. To cram in all the news, editors resorted to tiny, hard-to-read type. At the same time, goods produced in Israel for export had to be transported over great distances to find a market, which was hardly a way to keep prices competitive.

But adversity served as a unifying force. Even in the economically precarious years of the late 1940s and early 1950s, public morale remained high. Inspired by its first prime minister, David Ben-Gurion, the new nation set practical goals for itself: to conquer the desert, to build roads, factories and homes, to gather in the exiles. Above all, Israelis had to acquire a new self-image: They were no longer settlers, but owners of an independent state.

The excitement — and the discomforts — of those early years are vividly remembered by Edi Danino, now a prominent labor-union leader, whose family came to Israel from Morocco in 1956, when Edi was 17. "We prayed all

Outside a warehouse in the port of Ashdod, a truckdriver uncovers a shipment of lemons. Marketed under the Jaffa label, citrus fruit accounts for more than 30 percent of the country's agricultural exports.

our lives to live as free men in a Jewish state," he recalls. But the realities of Israel hit hard. On arrival, they were taken to an immigration center at Ramla, near Tel Aviv. Not far away was the valley where Joshua had ordered the sun and the moon to stand still. But the Biblical associations had little appeal for the family when they saw the accommodations assigned to them. Edi's father took one look at the shack they would have to live in during the oncoming winter and proudly announced, "Not one night will we sleep here." Whereupon he marched out of the camp with his wife, Edi and Edi's sister.

Fortunately, three other sons in the family had preceded them, and one had a single-room apartment. There the Daninos spent their first months in the country. Edi remembers how the beds were lined up head-to-foot around the walls of the single room. In the middle was a table and chairs where the family crowded together to eat the meals Edi's mother cooked on a single-burner kerosene stove.

Within three months, Edi was called to the army. "That gave the family a little more room. It was tough to adjust, but we were now in our own land and we felt we were building something new for ourselves and our people."

The Danino family, like many of their fellow newcomers to Israel in the 1950s, grumbled about the overcrowd-

ing, food shortages and many other inconveniences. But the public shared a powerful sense of purpose, and conversations that began with a litany of complaints usually ended with the words *"yi'hyeh tov"* — meaning "one day it will be good." In Edi's case, the improvement was not long in coming. After finishing his army service in 1959, he went to work as a tool mechanic at the large Middle East Pipe factory in Ramla and became active in the labor union there. Before long, he was well on the way to a powerful position as a worker-representative on the plant's board of directors.

The state developed swiftly. From Dan in the north to the new port of Eilat at the southernmost tip, roads, housing, factories and settlements were appearing almost overnight. It was common to hear people say, "I was here two weeks ago, but that building wasn't built then." While traveling in Israel, American television journalist Edward R. Murrow observed, "If the Star of David were not on the flag of Israel, the cement-mixer would be."

Integrating new arrivals was a high priority, but it proved expensive in both money and human resources. The public knew that even though national growth was increasing at an unprecedented 10 percent every year, enormous infusions of capital and time — at least a decade — would be required to achieve Western European living standards. No one expected to grow rich immediately. Indeed, it was — and still is — a common Israeli maxim: "If you want to make a small fortune in Israel, come with a large one."

But money was beginning to roll in. About $820 million came in the form of West German war reparations and restitution payments to individual Holocaust victims. Funds also came from the sale of Israel Bonds in the United States and from Jewish contributions throughout the world.

The growth in the 1950s continued unabated into the next decade; in fact, the early '60s saw a boom period of rising exports and increasing prosperity. New industries were opening up, while slightly older enterprises began to flourish: Textiles and leather goods, copper mining, electronics, diamond cutting and petrochemical production were all rising to profitable heights, and Israelis reaped the benefits of their early hard work and sacrifices.

But even as they celebrated their successes, some Israelis expressed concern about the size of the national debt and about the steady outflow of funds for expensive imports — raw materials as well as consumer goods — which continued to exceed export sales. Optimistic economists, however, predicted that, if the current growth rates were maintained, Israel would be able to free itself from its vast payments deficit by the early 1970s.

The Six Day War of 1967 cast a shadow over these rosy prognostications. Defense spending and the production of military equipment took precedence over the manufacture of goods for export, and currency poured out of the country at a prodigious rate for the purchase of more arms abroad.

The economy recovered rapidly after the war, with full employment, a hefty increase in tourism — caused largely by foreign Jews visiting a newly reunited Jerusalem and the reclaimed Western Wall — and renewed industrial expansion. Immigration, which had previously been on the wane, suddenly increased, with an influx from the prosperous West. But the nation was still spending an inordinate amount on its defense, and these costs spiraled even higher in the early years of the 1970s as a consequence of the 1973 Yom Kippur War. At the same time, the nation found itself sharing the economic woes that were plaguing the whole Western world: Soaring global inflation and the

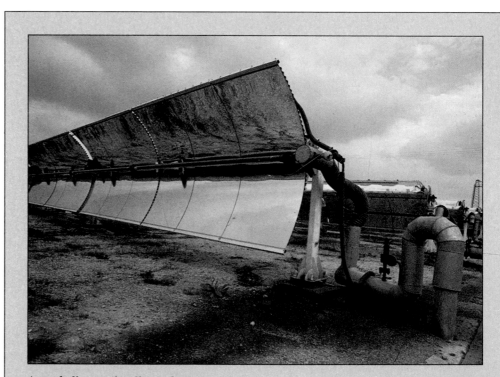

A parabolic-trough collector focuses sunlight onto heat-absorption pipes containing a fluid capable of reaching temperatures higher than 570° F. Once hot, the fluid is circulated to a boiler and heat exchanger, producing steam, which in turn generates electricity.

Covered with netting to increase surface tension and reduce evaporation, a solar pond filters sunlight through layers of increasingly salty water, heating the brine at the bottom to the boiling point. Too saturated with salt to rise, the dense, trapped liquid becomes a heat reservoir, storing energy.

energy crisis only compounded the nation's own financial problems.

In spite of an economic situation that grew increasingly unstable in the early years of the 1980s, Israelis who, like Edi Danino, had grown up with the new state could point to signs of solid material progress in every aspect of their daily lives. In the 1950s, for example, Israel had only 31,000 private telephones. By 1984, this figure had increased to 1.6 million. Between 1950 and the mid-1980s, private cars had increased in number by 6,000 percent; by 1985, they traveled along more than 7,800 miles of roads, some of them six-lane highways. Sadly, however, the negative side of growth also showed itself on the roads; between 1982 and 1984, for instance, there were nearly three times as many traffic fatalities as there were war deaths in Lebanon during the same period.

Nowhere is Israel's economic progress more conspicuous than in agriculture. Long before statehood, the nation's founders knew that their first priority was to improve the land — to feed themselves and the waves of immigrants they hoped would follow.

One of the prime movers of these endeavors was a farmer — part Iraqi, part Russian — named Ezra Danin, son of one of the founders of Tel Aviv. Born in 1902, he abandoned a short-lived career as a public official in order to study farming; he dedicated himself to a life on the land. Of physically imposing character, tall and heavily built, he was celebrated among his friends for his prodigious appetite for good food, and he was respected by his fellow farmers — Arabs as well as Jews — for his efforts to increase their prosperity.

Danin's farmhouse at Hadera, which was halfway between Tel Aviv and Haifa, was a center of agricultural experimentation and innovation. Danin and his colleagues pondered the problem of developing Palestine for the good of all its inhabitants.

Their approach was simple. They had to start by improving the soil. To do this, they needed to find new sources of water, rarest of raw materials, and they had to learn how to use it as economically as possible. They tried to grow crops that consumed little water — apples, for instance, were rejected as a possibility because the water they used up could not be compensated for by the nourishment they provided. Farmers tried to grow profit-making fruit and vegetables for export and to produce for themselves those essentials — such as animal feed — that would otherwise have to be imported.

The work could not be done, however, without first educating the people involved — not only the farmers but also the government officials who made and applied the relevant policies. Danin had great faith in farmers but much less in bureaucrats and planners, with their enthusiasm for large, expensive and impractical schemes.

Over a period of 50 years, spanning the British mandate and the establishment of the state, Danin tackled an extraordinarily wide range of problems in husbandry, from experiments with

TAPPING ENERGY FROM THE SUN

Sunshine is a plentiful natural resource in Israel, and even before the energy crisis of the 1970s, Israeli scientists were experimenting with ways of harnessing solar power to produce electricity.

Per capita, the Israelis are now the world's largest consumers of solar energy, and the search for new ways to use the sun's power continues. Projects now in progress include a pipeline that will carry solar energy over long distances and a solar cell with enough storage capacity to continue to produce energy after dark.

5

crop species to fish farming. He met with groups of farmers and officials and convinced them that water and education could help even those working small farms to double or triple their crop — and, subsequently, their standard of living.

Danin also provided Israel with one of its most important exports — agricultural expertise. Even when foreign relations with many Third World nations were impossible in diplomatic terms, there was hardly a developing African or Asian state that did not seek Israeli help to solve problems that had been tackled in the farmhouse at Hadera.

What Danin taught and others emulated was a national approach to eco-

nomic requirements that would also integrate the needs of the individual. He and his colleagues set Israeli agriculture on course with the injunction: "Enrich the country, and if you can, enrich also yourselves."

The planning, investment, mechanization and water engineering advocated by Ezra Danin from the 1920s to the 1970s has paid off. Today, the kibbutzim, the moshavim and the smaller number of independent farmers collectively produce more than enough food for the population. The nation now earns 10 percent of its income from agricultural exports.

Farms yield bountiful crops of citrus fruit, avocados, bananas, celery, broc-

coli, corn, wheat, pecans, persimmons and flowers. Israeli poultry farmers raise chickens, geese and turkeys, and even ostriches.

Some agricultural innovations have been the result of luck rather than planning, of help by the right people turning up at the right time. In 1952, for instance, a California farmer named Sam Hamburg visited Israel for a reunion with long-lost relatives. During his stay, he was introduced to David Ben-Gurion. When the prime minister discovered that Hamburg was an expert in cotton production, he urged him to come to Israel and start a cotton farm in the Negev. "You grow the cotton, Hamburg, and we'll build the

Camels stand penned outside the Veterinary Institute for Comparative Medicine, where research is being conducted into breeding the animals for use as a source of meat. The institute is part of the Ben-Gurion University of the Negev, a world leader in arid-zone research.

textile factories," said Ben-Gurion.

The Californian was doubtful. The thin soil of the Negev was useless for growing cotton. But when Army Chief of Staff Yigael Yadin took him to the Bet She'an Valley, in the north near the Sea of Galilee, Hamburg changed his mind. "We don't have soil this good in California," he said.

Returning to the United States, he hired a water engineer, then traveled back to Israel 10 days later. Using conscripted soldiers provided by Yadin as workers, Hamburg planted an experimental crop with spectacular results. In little more than a decade, Israel's fully mechanized cotton fields were producing more than its newly built textile mills could handle, and Israel became a cotton exporter.

By the mid-1980s, cotton had become the country's second major crop, outstripped only by citrus fruit. The white bolls now cover more than 133,000 acres, from the Golan Heights to the northern Negev. Production has been so intensive that Israel leads the world in yield per acre.

Most of Israel's cotton is produced by the nation's 270 kibbutzim, which yield 45 percent of Israel's agricultural products. Following the tradition of improvisation and experimentation handed down by their founders, kibbutz farms are among the world's most innovative agricultural establishments. Many crops are watered by the computer-programmed drip-irrigation systems pioneered by kibbutz farmers. Their fish farms, based on artificial ponds with controlled environments, supply record amounts of fresh-water fish. Kibbutz-produced carp, mullet and St. Peter's fish, named after the Biblical fisherman, provide one quarter of all the fish served on Israeli tables.

Seasonal workers harvest oranges on a moshav — a farming cooperative where villagers own their homes and work individual plots but market crops collectively. Each moshav houses about 60 families, sharing profits, machinery and responsibilities.

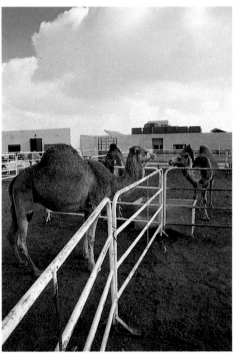

High technology has become part of the fabric of kibbutz life. One settlement, for example, faced with the task of providing 3,600 meals daily in its communal dining room, has developed software to program its menus for a year in advance. Every morning, kibbutz members on kitchen duty receive a print-out with all the information they need, including recipes, to prepare and serve the day's food.

On many kibbutzim, high technology has eclipsed farming as a source of income. Today, half of Israel's industrial robots are made in kibbutz workshops, as are many of the solar-energy collectors that heat Israeli homes.

Other kibbutzim have entered the hotel business, to take advantage of the many foreign visitors who make tourism one of Israel's largest industries.

There are kibbutz inns that boast Olympic-size swimming pools and tournament-standard tennis courts. A luxury hotel on a kibbutz produces some incongruities: vacationers, sunbathing in bikinis or sipping gin and tonic on the lawn within sight of others hard at work in boots and overalls, mucking out cowsheds and pitching hay. But, according to Uri Yanai, a bookkeeper at Kibbutz Ein Gev, which serves St. Peter's fish in its Sea of Galilee restaurant and hires out recreational vehicles, this does not trouble the kibbutzniks. "The tourists are now competing with the banana crop."

Like the kibbutzim, the moshavim have extended the range of their activities into manufacturing and retailing. One cooperative, for instance, has supplemented its income by establishing a roadside shop that sells salami and art posters.

The changes in the kibbutzim and moshavim reflect developments in the nation as a whole. Few of its people now look to the land for their livelihood. Eleven percent of the work force was employed in agriculture in 1950. By the mid-1980s, the number had dropped to only 5.4 percent.

Ninety percent of all Israeli workers belong to the giant organization officially titled the General Federation of Labor, but universally known as the Histadrut. Through its manifold industrial, financial, union and welfare activities, the Histadrut is the single most influential force in the Israeli economy. Controlling 43 national, professional and occupational unions, the Histadrut stands behind almost every paycheck in the nation; the Histadrut's Tel Aviv headquarters is jokingly referred to by Israelis as "the Kremlin."

5

The Histadrut began in 1920, when 87 workers met in the port city of Haifa to establish an organization that would unite Jewish labor, in preparation for the creation of the Jewish commonwealth. It was a time when thousands of young Eastern European settlers were flocking to Palestine, inspired by the exhortations of the Zionist leader Joseph Trumpeldor, who declared, "I am not tied by anything — I know only one rule: Build."

The young radicals formed voluntary labor brigades to construct the roads for a new Jewish homeland. Thirty years later many of these same laborers would take it upon themselves to build a government; Ben-Gurion and other political leaders and labor unionists had all, in their youth, served their time on the road gangs.

Fueled by the energy of its founders and their grand plans for nationalizing, the Histadrut became builder and paver, financier and banker, employer and employee, insurer and pension-giver, doctor and nurse. It simultaneously fought for workers' rights and provided seed money and personnel for new enterprises. By becoming owner and controller of the state's major industries, it not only consolidated the power of the Israeli work force, but virtually shaped the economic life of the country. Because its priorities were development and job creation rather than pure profit, it often stepped in where private investors feared to tread.

Cushioned by a staggering array of welfare benefits, the workers of the Histadrut participate on an equal footing with management in the running of this important empire. Its diverse enterprises generate 25 percent of Israel's gross national product, and run the gamut from banking and book publishing to the national bus line, Egged.

The Histadrut's huge construction company, Solel Boneh (meaning "Pavers and Builders"), accounts for a similar percentage of the country's building activities. During World War II, it built roads and airfields for the British forces throughout the Middle East and Africa, and since that time, it has been responsible for domestic projects ranging from superhighways to a Roman Catholic basilica. Abroad, its engineers have directed the construction of a NATO airport in Turkey, a bridge in Nepal, dams in Nigeria, a cement plant in Togo and an entire town hacked out of the jungle in the Ivory Coast.

Another Histadrut enterprise, Koor Industries, is a holding company employing 35,000 workers. Starting in 1945 as a manufacturer of bricks and plumbing fixtures, Koor played its part in the War of Independence. The Jewish forces, desperately short of defensive weapons and vehicles, asked Koor to armor civilian trucks and buses so they could be used to carry supplies through heavy gunfire to besieged fighters in Jerusalem. Some of the converted civilian supply vehicles never made it, and their steel bodies, sculpted by artillery fire, still stand beside Route 1 between Jerusalem and Tel Aviv. Today, Koor produces everything from pipes to plastics to pilotless planes.

Israel Aircraft Industries, Israel's largest corporation, also developed out of conflict. During the War of Independence, a polio-stricken 30-year-old American named Al Schwimmer, formerly a World War II flight engineer, traveled the world in search of tools and spare parts to build an air defense for the embattled nation. Undeterred by an American embargo on shipments of arms and equipment to the Middle

A CENTER FOR SCIENTIFIC EXCELLENCE

Lacking the natural resources of other countries, Israel has sought prosperity by developing advanced science and high-tech industries. It now has the highest percentage of research and development personnel in the world.

Most Israelis in this field have been educated at, or work for, the Technion in Haifa, the country's oldest institution of higher learning, founded in 1912. In addition to teaching 6,000 undergraduates, the Technion has its own research foundation. Projects — funded by the government, industry and foreign sponsors — range from alternative energy sources and genetic engineering to robotics and laser technology. Medical research, spurred by the needs of Israel's war wounded, is also undertaken.

At the Technion Medical School, a sleeping child's recorded brain activity is observed. The school investigates problems such as insomnia and chronic sleepiness and studies the role of sleep in preventive medicine.

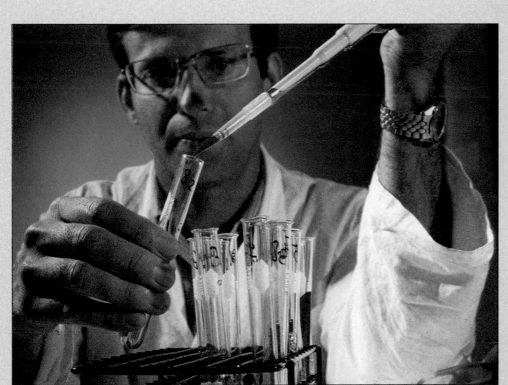

A scientist places a blood sample in a test tube at the Technion's Biomaterials Laboratory; research is being done into developing artificial blood and plasma that can be stored unrefrigerated. The chief purpose of the project is to improve facilities for casualties in time of war.

A biomedical engineer fits an artificial arm to a test model. An increase in the number of amputees, brought about by the 1973 Yom Kippur War, has stimulated the development of advanced artificial limbs, including one type that informs its wearer of movements by means of electronic impulses.

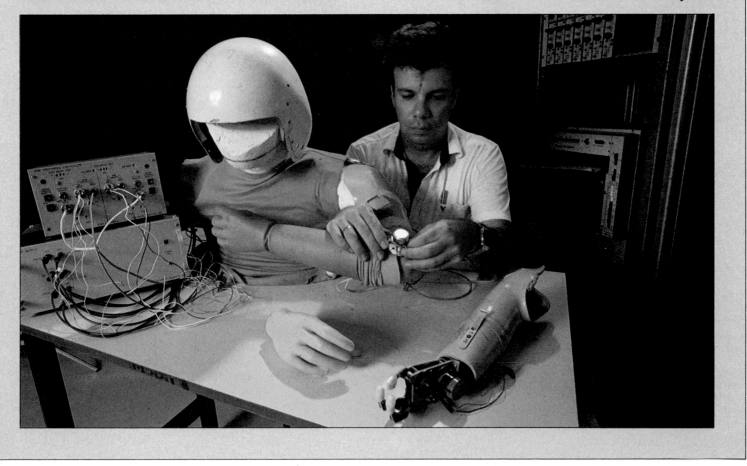

5

East, Schwimmer gathered a fleet of used Curtiss C-46 Commandos and Lockheed Constellations at his aviation maintenance workshop in California. He dismantled the planes and crated them to Panama where — so he announced — he was setting up a new commercial airline. Once in Panama, the aircraft were reassembled and flown to Israel.

Schwimmer's planes provided the start for the new Israeli air force and, later, for the commercial airline El Al. Schwimmer himself, fined heavily by the U.S. government for violating the embargo, moved to Israel and set up an aircraft maintenance plant at Lod, Israel's new international airport. By the 1980s, his company had expanded into an industrial giant, producing state-of-the-art jet fighters and missiles, as well as aircraft for more pacific purposes, such as executive jets.

Because Israel's weapons systems have been so thoroughly tested on the battlefield, they find ready purchasers throughout the world. An early commercial success in the 1960s was the Uzi submachine gun, followed by advanced fighter planes, missile boats, a new type of fire-resistant battle tank and electronic fences to foil clandestine border crossings. By the 1980s, Israel had reportedly become one of the major armaments exporters in the world, ranked closely behind Italy, the United Kingdom and West Germany. Even nations that do not maintain diplomatic relations with Israel discreetly order its military products.

Much of Israel's high-technology research, however, is directed to more peaceful uses. Israeli scientists have created new products and processes in communications, graphics reproduction, microcomputers and medical

technology. One electronics company, for example, has developed a new diagnostic system known as nuclear imaging. This process produces detailed cross-sectional images of the body and simultaneously measures the average chemical composition of body tissue. The system can pick up changes in tissue chemistry that would not be visible in electronic scans, and it has none of the radiation risks associated with conventional X-rays.

Less dramatic, perhaps, than nuclear imaging but likely to bring relief to millions, is the rhinotherm, developed at the Weizmann Institute of Science. By delivering concentrated doses of heated air to the nose and the sinuses, the

rhinotherm inhibits the growth of the viruses that cause nasal congestion and sneezing. Its advocates describe it as the closest thing yet found to a cure for the common cold.

Nearly 6 percent of the Israeli work force is employed in these and other high-technology industries; another 30 percent earn their living in public and community services. But no matter what sector of the economy an Israeli works in, one of the more perplexing aspects is the paycheck, colloquially known as the *loksh*, or "noodle," because it is long and thin. These checks are less than half an inch wide but sometimes reach a length of two feet,

GIFTS FROM FRIENDS ABROAD

One of the first things that a visitor to Israel notices is the number of plaques commemorating foreign individuals or organizations that have contributed funds or amenities to the state. Inscriptions can be seen on hospitals, ambulances, student hostels, park entrances — even on the backs of chairs *(right)* given for the use of pilgrims at Jerusalem's Western Wall.

Indeed, the financial support of Diaspora Jewry has been crucial to the establishment and economic survival of Israel. By far the largest single source of funds is the United Israel Appeal, to which American Jews alone contributed more than four billion dollars between 1948 and 1986.

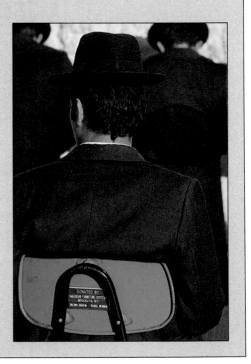

128

and they are as difficult to disentangle as a mound of spaghetti.

A typical example is the monthly paycheck received by Joseph Neipris, a senior lecturer at the Hebrew University's School of Social Work in Jerusalem. On the income side, there are no fewer than 15 separate items: included among them are Neipris' basic salary; seniority pay and an advance on a salary increase currently in arbitration; the bus fare to the campus (three minutes away from his home); an allowance for automobile ownership, something called "reimbursement for car expenses," as well as an advance on a car-allowance increase also under negotiation; "erosion" supplements to make up for losses from inflation on both basic and seniority pay; a telephone allowance; an additional unspecified 4 percent allowance ("I'm not sure what that's for," admits Neipris); and, finally, three supplements for research expenses representing 5 percent, 9 percent and 25 percent respectively of his basic salary.

The deductions on the paycheck are smaller in number but substantial in size: income tax; national insurance; sick fund; two obligatory savings funds; dues for membership in an academic organization; university life insurance; and funds for advanced study abroad. Once these deductions have been made, Neipris has slightly more than half his basic salary left to take home.

In compensation, however, he receives the benefits of a wide-ranging social security system that cares for Israelis from cradle to grave, providing everything from substantial maternity grants to free cemetery plots. The system also offers generous disability insurance and pays the salaries of workers released for army reserve duty — which is a considerable drain on the public purse since many members of the work force may be on active duty at any one time.

In order to pay for it all, the Israeli worker carries one of the heaviest tax burdens in the world. On the average, half of all personal income returns to the government in the form of tax. Besides taxing earnings, the treasury slaps a substantial value-added tax on all goods and services. Compulsory car deposits are another source of revenue: When Israelis buy a car, they must deposit a sum with the treasury — in some years, as much as 40 percent of the car's purchase price — to be returned to the depositor, without interest, 12 months later.

Because the tax load has always been heavy, it is common practice for employers to offer their workers a glittering array of perks and fringe benefits. Some payroll departments display a considerable amount of ingenuity: One electronics engineer, for instance, says that for many years his company paid him a generous "rent" for the space his private telephone occupied in his home. Many workers receive car allowances even if they do not own a car, while others are rewarded with a company car or grants for books and clothing. Professors are given free tuition for their children; electricity workers get free electricity for their

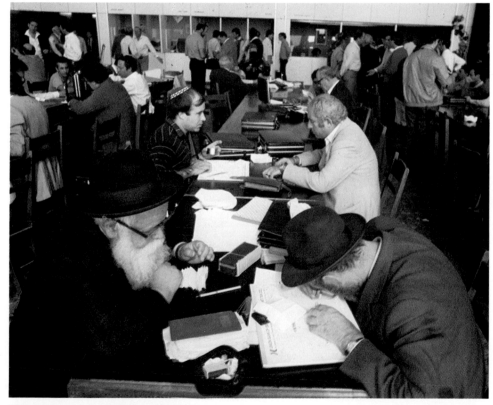

Gem traders conduct business at the Israel Diamond Exchange at Ramat Gan in Tel Aviv, center of the country's largest export industry. Among the 1,600 members of the exchange, multimillion-dollar deals are matters of trust — sealed with a casually uttered *"mazal,"* Hebrew for "luck."

5

homes. Since 1975, most of these benefits have been taxed, but they have become institutionalized as an integral part of the wage structure.

In effect, wage policy is determined by the government. As the country's single largest employer — with one third of the nation's work force on its payroll — the state controls the labor market. Once the government agrees to a higher pay scale for one group of workers — teachers, for example — a ripple effect takes place, with other groups of workers, from physicians to postal clerks, asking for commensurate pay raises. The demand for parity then spreads to private industry.

In the 1980s, Israeli salaries, like those of workers throughout the world, were sharply affected by inflation. For many years some cushioning was provided by the system of index-linking: At regular intervals workers received cost-of-living allowances in line with the current inflation rate. However, their expenditures were also index-linked, which of course meant corresponding rises in life-insurance premiums, electricity bills and other charges.

In part, Israel's inflation problems could be seen as local effects from a global financial crisis. But they were also symptoms of an overheated economy that was rapidly heading for a blowout. In addition to record-breaking inflation rates, the beginning of the 1980s saw foreign-currency reserves shrinking at an alarming rate and economic growth coming to a standstill.

But even more worrisome was an enormous foreign debt. In 1984, for example, every man, woman and child in Israel owed foreign creditors — principally the government of the United States — almost $7,000, the largest per capita debt of any nation in the world.

In a country that was accustomed to full employment, unemployment had begun to rise. Some normally healthy branches of the economy were foundering or failing. The construction industry was near collapse as the government was forced to cut its building program. The country's first textile factory was on the verge of bankruptcy. Banks, usually the source of huge profits, were reporting losses. Worse still, the public had lost faith in Israeli currency — the shekel — and shops were quoting prices in American dollars. After years of apparent prosperity, the nation discovered that affluence was an illusion.

Some economists had been warning of impending disaster since the boom years of the 1960s. By 1983, leading economist Haim Ben-Shachar concluded, "This fool's paradise has to end." And end it did. On the farms, as in the towns, Israelis asked themselves "What has gone wrong?"

Since independence, pressures from within and without had forced Israel to grow at a speed that far outstripped its resources. Year after year, the country spent beyond its means to pay. But the nation's leaders had determined that survival demanded the swift build-up of a superior defense force, full employment and the rapid integration of an immigrant population. As early as 1949, a Jerusalem newspaper editor had expressed the belief that "Melting pot methods take too long. We've got to be a pressure cooker."

By collecting resources from abroad, through the establishment of an organization to sell development bonds, by borrowing heavily from banks and governments, by accepting — with some reluctance — restitution and reparations payments from Germany, and by depriving its citizens of all but their most elementary needs, the pressure cooker built up steam. From 1949 to 1972, the growth rate averaged 10 percent; in the meantime, real income per capita increased at a rate varying between 4 and 5 percent.

Near the place where Lot's wife was turned into a pillar of salt, a pile of potash stands outside a Dead Sea processing plant. Since Biblical times, people have exploited the mineral wealth of the world's most saline sea, with its estimated 49 trillion tons of salts.

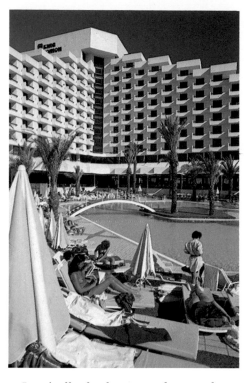

On a typical January day in Eilat, tourists relax at the poolside of one of the resort's most luxurious hotels. Israel's warm climate, religious sites and archeological treasures attract more than one million tourists annually.

Ironically, both war and peace have been heavy drains on, as well as powerful stimuli to, the economy. The 1973 Yom Kippur War disrupted the economy by involving it in huge defense spending. The 1979 peace treaty with Egypt entailed the construction of new defense lines and air bases. The total cost, directly and indirectly, to Israel as a result of the move from Sinai, has not been revealed. One economist involved in a government study suggests the price may have been "in the billions of dollars," even greater than that of the early 1980s war in Lebanon.

Together with military expenditure, which always accounted for the lion's share of Israel's expenses, private spending soared in the late '70s. In 1977, the government, led by Menachem Begin, liberated the economy, encouraged higher consumer spending, allowed Israelis to hold foreign currency and increased the standard of living far beyond the public's genuine ability to afford it. The value of the shekel was kept artificially high, and taxes were reduced on imported goods.

The public went on a frantic shopping spree, motivated by the assertions of politicians that "you never had it so good." The purchasing of videos, swimming pools and other luxury items became a national craze. "I bought a video," admits Edi Danino, "because all my neighbors were getting them." During the same period of time, he also acquired a freezer, a color television set and a new refrigerator.

He was not alone. One Jerusalem woman admitted to a shop assistant that she was buying a vacuum cleaner even though she had no rugs in her house. "I might as well take advantage," she explained. "One day I may buy rugs, too."

Imported foods were selling in the supermarkets at prices that were much lower than local produce, with devastating effects on Israeli farmers.

In the Negev, the moshavim were in a state of panic. Agricultural cooperatives that had burgeoned in the area were losing their domestic and international customers as their citrus fruit, flowers and tomatoes became less and less competitive on the export market. As their debts mounted, the amount of aid they could expect from a hard-pressed government decreased. In desperation, many farmers uprooted their orange groves. Tourism within the country also suffered, as Israelis decided it was cheaper to take their vacations abroad than at home.

Money flowed out of Israel at a high rate, using up foreign-currency reserves faster than they could be replaced. At the same time, the country went deeper into debt as the treasury printed mountains of money to pay bills, further weakening the shekel.

The major military build-up, the liberalized economy and uncontrolled

5

consumption, combined with stagnant growth, resulted in an inflation rate that at one point reached a horrific 1,000 percent. As the shekel plummeted in value, eroding at a rate of 2 percent a day, Israelis bought American dollars, put their shekels into dollar-linked savings accounts, or safeguarded their paychecks by investing in high-interest, income tax-free bank accounts for periods of a week or two.

"Every Israeli was to be his own financial consultant," said one young computer technician. "The sort of ordinary worker who used to open his newspaper at the sports pages now goes straight to the financial columns, so he can figure out what he ought to do with his money next."

The loss of confidence in the shekel created a huge "black money" market — dollars on which no taxes were paid — that was estimated to run into the billions. Israelis told stories of friends who were buying dollars by the bushel and stuffing the bills into their mattresses or under the floor tiles.

Late in 1983, the crisis headed toward catastrophe. The banks began to run out of cash, and the Tel Aviv stock market was closed down for five days to avert financial disaster. The government took emergency steps to rescue the banks and relieve the crisis of confidence, but the measures were only temporary and the basic problems remained: out-of-control inflation, an unrealistically high standard of living, unalleviated government spending, low foreign-currency reserves and an enormous foreign debt.

Economic security became top priority for Israelis as the awful truth hit home. The continuing crisis precipitated early elections in the summer of 1984, and after long political negotia-

tions, a national coalition government took office. Its prime minister, Shimon Peres, a protégé of David Ben-Gurion, stated, "We will not permit the increase in the standard of living to exceed the increase in production." Peres enforced stern measures, including a temporary freeze on wages and prices, a ban on a wide range of imports and plans for a massive reduction in government spending. Israelis tightened their belts for a period of austerity. And for the first time, they faced the prospect of high unemployment.

The resulting shock affected every Israeli. Edi Danino, for instance, found himself, at the end of 1984, spending long nights in meetings with the management of the Middle East Pipe Company, trying to find a formula for creating new jobs to avert dismissals. Inside the once-prosperous plant that made pipes for Israel's oil pipelines and for the National Water Carrier, machinery was strangely silent.

"We have taken one order from the U.S. at a financial loss, just to keep the men at their jobs," said Edi. "At home my son is now out of the army but can't find work, and I'm afraid he'll move abroad. My salary doesn't stretch to the end of the month any more, and my wife has started work as a checkout assistant in a supermarket to help make ends meet."

There were no simple economic solutions to the nation's problems. Quite apart from the fact that Israel was still not earning as much as it was spending, 26 percent of its income — the largest single item in the budget — went to repay creditors. In spite of its economic woes, Israel had never yet defaulted on a loan, and for that reason, its credit was still good.

The principal lender remains the

U.S. government. Over the years, the United States has given Israel at least $30 billion in financial aid, with the understanding that a large proportion of the money would be spent on U.S.-made goods and armaments. In 1984, American aid amounted to $2.6 billion; $1.2 billion of that was a grant to support the economy. Under normal circumstances, the United States doled out its aid in installments, but when Israel's reserves dropped precariously at the end of that year, the Americans advanced the entire $1.2 billion in one payment. The Americans also allocated $1.4 billion in military aid, which, for the first time, took the form of a grant rather than a loan.

The effect was salubrious, as Israel reported a steep rise in the Bank of Israel's foreign-currency account. The improved balance of payments figures, the wage and price freeze, and the government spending cuts all helped to restore some tranquillity to the economic community. But Israelis agreed that a major restructuring of the country's economy was necessary.

Some observers felt that the Israeli economy was far too dependent on American financial aid — which in 1985 amounted to $3.35 billion (with $1.9 billion as a support grant to Israel's economy) — and on the continued good will of the United States Congress. At the opposite end of the spectrum, however, were those economists who felt that, in the continuing struggle between the superpowers, Israel's strategic value to the United States far outweighed the amount of American aid actually received. According to this school of thought, the nation's payments for services rendered should be relative to the financial aid America gives to the NATO countries, which

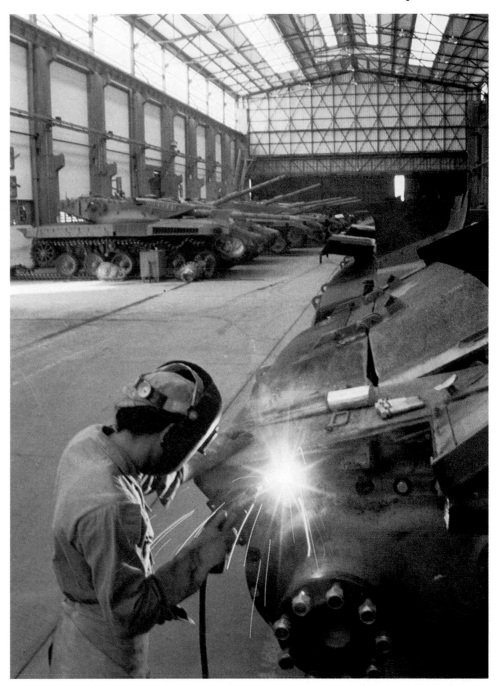

in the early 1980s were together receiving almost 40 times the amount granted to Israel.

Whatever shifts may occur in the tides of superpower politics, Israel's own, immediate defense needs remain a continuing strain on the nation's economy. Israel spends approximately $10 billion — nearly 30 percent of its budget — on defense, in comparison to an estimated $70 billion spent by the Arab states. But its citizens have become profoundly concerned about this continuing drain of human and financial resources and its impact on the economic future of the nation. In the strife-torn Middle East, lasting peace and true prosperity seem equally difficult to attain.

In the final analysis, Israelis accept that the healing of the economy must come not through copious doses of American aid but from Israel's own energy and ingenuity. The future of the state again depends upon the creativity of its pioneers, although in this generation, the fields they labor in are likely to be those of scientific research and new technology.

In this respect, the words David Ben-Gurion addressed to his own political party in 1960 are still pertinent today: "We have always been a small people, but this small people has occupied a greater place in world history than nations many times its size. We have enemies as no other nation has, and we have friends as no other nation has. Both of them make it necessary for us to undertake tremendous efforts, not only in security and international relations but also in the sphere of pioneering achievement; in the creation of a model society and the institution of revolutionary changes in the landscape and the economy of the country." □

HARD-WON WATER TO TRANSFORM A WILDERNESS

One of Israel's greatest challenges has been to provide enough food for its expanding population, and this, in turn, has triggered a massive and costly campaign to reclaim the Negev, the 5,400 square miles of sun-baked wilderness that make up 65 percent of the national land area. The initial prospects were hardly encouraging. With an annual rainfall of eight inches in the north and slightly more than one inch in the south, the Negev seemed more suited to scorpions and sand flies than to fruit growers and farmers.

The turning point in the reclamation effort came in 1964 with the completion of the Israeli National Water Carrier, an elaborate system of pipes, conduits and tunnels that was designed to carry water from the Sea of Galilee, in the far north, to the rain-starved areas of the center and the south. For the Negev itself, the project meant an additional 84.5 billion gallons of water a year — a 75 percent increase that gave new significance to the words of the Prophet Ezekiel, who spoke of a time when the desert would be traversed by a great river and claimed that "every thing shall live whither the river cometh." By 1985, some 150,000 acres were under cultivation and a onetime wasteland of sand and rock was yielding a rich crop of fruit, vegetables, grain and cotton.

Another vital element in the greening of the Negev has been the widespread use of new technology, especially drip irrigation, which reduces moisture loss by feeding controlled amounts of water directly to the plants' roots. But the key to long-term development lies deep beneath the desert, where vast deposits of ice-age water are buried. A small part of this underground reservoir has already been tapped, and like Ezekiel before them, Israeli scientists foresee the day when the whole great Negev will flow with life-giving water.

A farmer in the Negev catches water pumped from an aquifer — one of the underground reservoirs that are transforming the desert. Although such water is too salty to drink, it provides moisture for a variety of salt-resistant crops, from cotton to cucumbers.

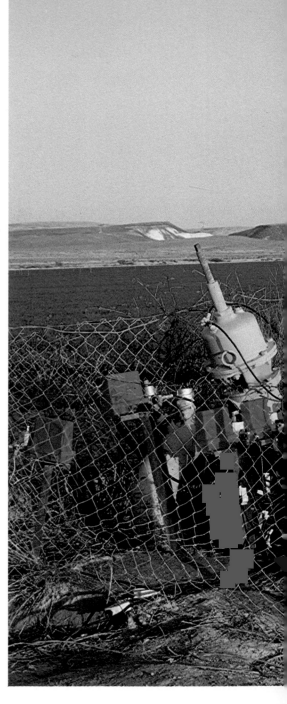

Broad-leaved agave and spiky yucca plants — the former yield an alcoholic beverage, the latter provide a soap base — are watered through hoses by drip irrigation. Developed in Israel in the 1960s, this technique is twice as economical in its use of water as the traditional sprinkler method.

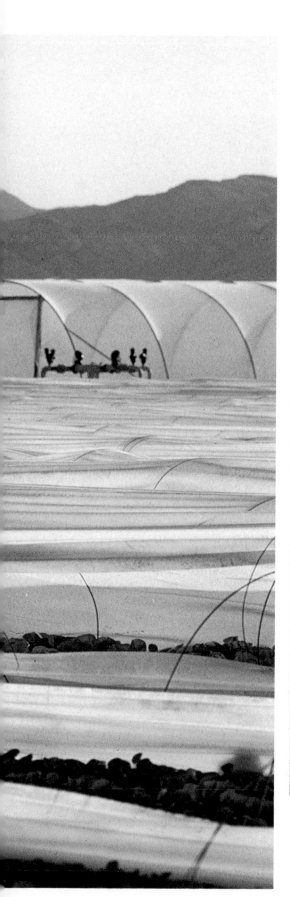

A farmer places plastic sheeting over a field of melons to prevent evaporation. Like the adjoining greenhouses, the field is heated and irrigated by pipes fed from the warm water of underground aquifers. This system ensures that the soil temperature will remain constant throughout the year.

An Arava Valley kibbutznik controls the irrigation of fields by computer, programmed to operate drip and sprinkler lines according to a preset sequence, which uses the available water with maximum efficiency. Such technology is playing a major part in the reclamation of the Negev.

Transformed by several days of intensive irrigation, a stretch of desert below the ruined Canaanite city of Arad is carpeted with burgeoning alfalfa. Drought remains a constant enemy, however, and any crops that did not receive adequate water would soon be swallowed by the encroaching sand.

142

BALANCING LAWS
OF GOD AND MAN

In a Beersheba square, a behatted member of the Lubavitch movement winds the leather straps of tefillin — a small box of sacred texts, worn during prayer — around the arm of a passerby. Lubavitchers strive to persuade non-observant Jews to return to religion.

Its Declaration of Independence guarantees freedom of religion to all inhabitants, but in the eyes of the world and in the minds of most of its own citizens, Israel is inescapably a Jewish state. In the simplest sense, the state is Jewish because 83 percent of its citizens are Jews; it exists in its present form partly because of the Zionist movement's efforts to establish a Jewish homeland in Palestine. But the nation's founders wanted Israel to be more than a place of refuge: They hoped that the new state would encourage and exemplify Jewish values of social justice and morality.

Human frailty notwithstanding, these aspirations might be easier to achieve if there were a consensus on the meaning of "Jewish values." But there is more than one Jewish world view: Jews, in Israel as elsewhere, run the gamut from devout believers, who adhere scrupulously to every syllable in the ancient canons of religious law, to atheists, who identify themselves as Jewish solely on the grounds of their ethnic origins.

Over the past 2,000 years, most of the Jews in the world remained faithful to the body of traditional laws and customs — the Halakah — and those who continue to do so now are known as Orthodox Jews. Since the 1800s, however, many Jews in Western nations have developed in different directions, and Judaism now has other branches: Reform Judaism seeks to adapt the religion to modern life, re-jecting such traditional practices as the separation of the sexes in the synagogue and the strict observance of the Sabbath as a day of rest. Conservatism, a more recent and largely American development, places itself in the middle ground, between the extremes of the Reform movement and the Orthodox. All three strands of Judaism are completely autonomous, with their own theological seminaries and religious congregations. While the two newer groups have a growing number of adherents in Israel, Orthodoxy remains the only form of Judaism officially recognized, and it has total control of Israel's powerful religious establishment.

Yet not even the Orthodox meet the exacting standards of piety and ritual purity that are demanded by the ultra-orthodox Haredim, who live mainly in Jerusalem's Mea Shearim quarter and in Bnei Brak, a township near Tel Aviv. The Haredim themselves are divided into several groups, although their lifestyles and clothes are superficially similar: Women wear modest, long-sleeved dresses, with wigs or scarves concealing their shaved heads; men wear long black overcoats and wide-brimmed velour hats on weekdays, and knee-breeches, fur-trimmed headgear and silk caftans on the Sabbath.

The most numerous are the Hasidim, followers of the Baal Shem Tov, an 18th-century teacher who rebelled against the excessive pedantry that then dominated Judaism. His emphasis

143

6

on serving the Lord with gladness attracted many followers. The movement flourished and grew in Eastern Europe and was carried far beyond its boundaries by emigrants. Hasidim traditionally stress deeds over Talmudic erudition, and they give their allegiance to one of several dynasties of *rebbes,* or saintly men, who are venerated as healers and miracle workers.

Fewer in number, but more powerful, are the Mitnagdim. Hard-line guardians of Jewish law, these devotees transferred to Israel the names and traditions of the great yeshivoth (religious academies) of Eastern Europe, destroyed by the Nazis.

The third major ultraorthodox group is the Yerushalmim, which is made up of families who have been in Jerusalem since the early 19th century and who were the largest group of Palestinian Jews before the arrival of the Zionists. Part of this community, living in Mea Shearim, call themselves Natorei Karta (Guardians of the Gate); they are militantly anti-Zionist, regarding the secular state as an abomination.

The Natorei Karta use Yiddish, not Hebrew, as the vernacular; they refuse to profane and debase the holy language by using it for anything other than prayer. They do not vote or take part in political life, and they will not cooperate with any state institution. From time to time, the Natorei Karta have even protested to the United Nations over such domestic issues as coed swimming in Jerusalem's pools, the performance of autopsies — which they see as a violation of religious law — and the desecration of ancient Jewish burial places by archeologists.

The guardians' resistance to the modern secular state is extreme. Nonetheless, for most Israelis, Jewish nationalism and the Jewish religion are inextricably intertwined. The relationship between them has always created intense debate and controversy, even in the 19th century, when the revival of Jewish statehood was no more than a dream. For religious Jews, only the coming of the Messiah would restore them to their ancestral homeland, and any attempt at human intervention was regarded as blasphemy.

For the Zionists, however, the only solution to the so-called Jewish problem — discrimination, persecution and oppression — was to preempt the Messiah's coming and set up a Jewish state as quickly as possible. But what kind of state? The founder of political Zionism, Theodor Herzl, asked in his trailblazing pamphlet *Der Judenstaat (The Jewish State):* "Shall we end up having a theocracy?" Herzl answered his own question with a firm negative, declaring, "We shall keep our rabbis within their synagogues, just as we shall keep our armies inside their barracks."

Such a view did little to encourage religious support, and the new movement, led by Westernized, secular and often socialist Jews, was shunned by most traditionalists. But the more moderate of them moved closer after the Second Zionist Congress of 1898, which resolved that "Zionism will not undertake to do anything contrary to the injunctions of the Jewish religion." A religious party called Mizrachi — an abbreviation of two Hebrew words meaning "spiritual center" — was formed; after statehood it became the National Religious Party (NRP).

Nevertheless, leadership of the Zionist movement remained with the nonreligious socialists. When the State of Israel was proclaimed, there was no doubt that the spirit of Theodor Herzl still inspired his successors. The state was not to be a theocracy. Its Declaration of Independence affirmed that it "would be based on freedom, justice and peace as envisaged by the prophets of Israel" and would guarantee freedom of religion. How emphatically secular the state intended to be was made clear when the religious representatives on the drafting committee failed, after much argument, to win majority support for their attempt to include a reference to God in the document.

It was a portent of things to come that the very birth of the state should be accompanied by this dispute over a religious issue. From the beginning, the life of modern-day Israel has rarely been free of religious controversies. Occasionally these have developed into political crises. The state may be secular officially, but its multiparty electoral system makes it possible for minority parties — especially the religious groups — to wield power that is out of proportion to the number of votes they actually receive.

A general election must be held in Israel at least every four years, and Article 4 of the Knesset Law of 1958 provides that this body shall be elected "by general, national, direct, equal, secret and proportional elections." All of Israel is one constituency, and the electors vote not for individuals but for a list of candidates presented by each party. The total number of votes cast is divided by 120 (the number of parliamentary seats), giving a figure that is the price, as it were, for each elected candidate. In the 1984 election, for example, the number of votes required to elect one member of the Knesset was 20,733.

This system offers a lot of possibilities for small parties. In any type of election based on a number of constituencies with a "first-off-the-mark" winner, small parties might never gain enough support in any one constituency to succeed. They have a much better chance of collecting enough votes throughout the whole country to win one or two seats. In the 1984 election, for instance, no fewer than 13 small parties received sufficient votes to send from one to five of their candidates to the Knesset to join the representations of the two major groups, the right-wing Likud and the left-wing Labor-Mapam Alignment (later named the Israel Labor Party). These two bodies are themselves alliances of formerly separate political parties.

Throughout the history of the state, such fragmentation has meant that no single party has won enough seats to ensure it an absolute parliamentary majority. The party with the largest number of Knesset members has to ne-

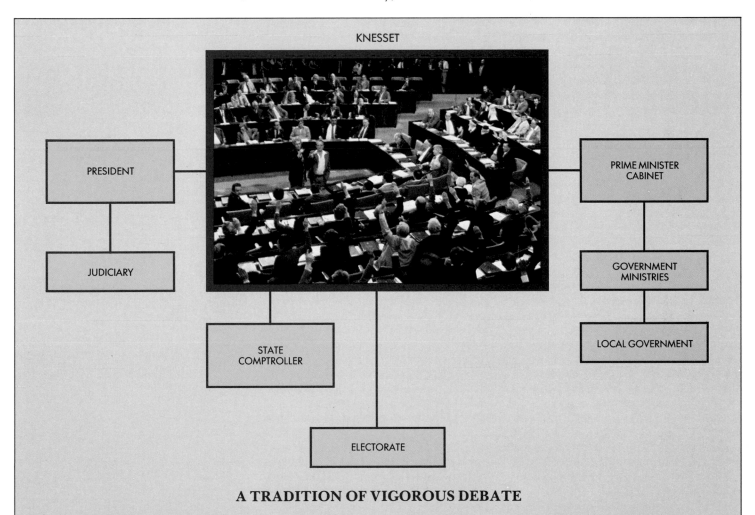

KNESSET

PRESIDENT

JUDICIARY

STATE COMPTROLLER

ELECTORATE

PRIME MINISTER CABINET

GOVERNMENT MINISTRIES

LOCAL GOVERNMENT

A TRADITION OF VIGOROUS DEBATE

Israel's parliament, the Knesset (Hebrew for "assembly"), stands at the heart of a turbulent but democratic political system. The Knesset's 120 members are elected every four years on the basis of strict proportional representation. The populace votes for parties, of which there are more than 20, rather than for individuals: The more votes cast for a party, the more seats it will hold in the Knesset.

The government, usually a coalition of a major party — Likud or Labor — and some of the small but powerful religious parties, is led by a prime minister, who selects the 25 Cabinet members. These head the various government departments, among them the Ministry of the Interior, which supervises local and regional councils.

The only person elected directly by the Knesset is the *nasi* (president). He, in turn, appoints judges, ambassadors and the state comptroller, who oversees the budgets and operations of all public bodies and is answerable to the Knesset alone.

6

146

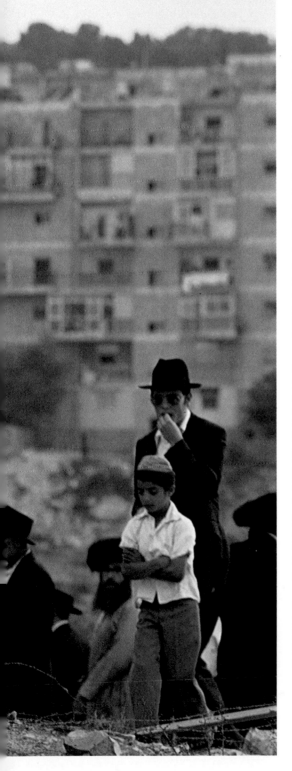

Angry Hasidic Jews gather by the road near their homes in the Mea Shearim quarter of Jerusalem to hurl stones at cars being driven on the Sabbath. The ultraorthodox sect's opposition to secular activities over this holy period has often led to violent confrontations.

gotiate with some of the smaller parties to form a coalition government. Those parties not included in the coalition collectively form the parliamentary opposition. In the first eight Israeli elections, the Labor-Mapam Alignment won the most seats and organized the coalitions. The results of the ninth and 10th, in 1977 and 1981, made the right-wing Likud group, headed by Menachem Begin, the dominant party.

The 1984 election, however, produced a change in the pattern. In this election as well, neither Labor, with 44 seats, nor the Likud, with 41 seats, could hope to form a government on its own. With the country facing the worst economic crisis in its history and with Israeli forces embroiled in Lebanon, the two rival groups came together to form a government of national unity. (The only other coalition of this kind was formed during the Six Day War of 1967.)

After each election, then, the business of coalition begins. The leaders of the small parties present their terms and begin to haggle: What favors will you do for us if we join you and help you form a government? From the point of view of the large parties, the religious parties have always been the most satisfactory of junior allies: Not being primarily concerned with the secular fields of foreign affairs, defense and the economy, they have usually been willing to give the coalition leader almost a free hand on these issues in return for government support of their special religious interests.

Israel has no formal, comprehensive constitution. It was decided, in the first years of the state, that the essential elements of a constitution should be formulated as a series of Basic Laws, enacted separately, that would eventually provide the constitution for the state. These Basic Laws cover such areas as the role of the president, the function of the Knesset, the machinery of government and the definition of Israel's lands. The Knesset as a whole votes on these and all other major and minor statutes, and it approves the policies put forward by the Cabinet.

Cabinet ministers — members of the Knesset drawn from the coalition parties — take responsibility for particular policy portfolios and government ministries. Two ministries, those of Religious Affairs and the Interior, are the traditional preserve of the religious parties: They are run by party members, who make sure that the key posts are filled by like-minded colleagues. Through the Ministry of Religious Affairs, the National Religious Party is able to exercise control of the religious establishments and administers a rich source of patronage in the distribution of funds to religious institutions.

The Ministry of the Interior is similarly able to make grants that benefit religious activities. It also provides the link between central government and local authorities: the municipal councils that run the cities and large towns, and the local and regional councils that run villages and rural areas. These bodies are governed by democratically elected councilors, who are responsible for managing the essential services for their communities: schools; health and social services; road maintenance; sewage, water-supply and other facilities, which are funded by a combination of local taxes and government grants. The Ministry of the Interior exercises control over council budgets and also supervises their overall administration. More important from the Orthodox point of view, this ministry also controls

6

matters of nationality, religion and marital status, covering all Israeli citizens alike, whether Jews or non-Jews.

By virtue of their bargaining power in the Knesset and their control over the relevant ministries, the religious parties have secured government backing for legislation to enforce religious observances and have ensured the continuation of a separate religious educational system; they have also maintained the monopoly of Orthodoxy as Israel's only officially recognized form of Judaism. Reform and Conservative Jews, mainly immigrants from Western nations, have repeatedly pressed for recognition of their movements by the Ministry of Religious Affairs and, just as often, have been refused it. The ministry has frequently offered to give these groups the status of separate religions, placing them in the same category as Christianity or Islam. But each time, the proposals have been firmly rejected by indignant representatives of both movements.

Although it maintains departments run by Muslims and Christians to serve the non-Jewish communities and provide support for their ritual needs and religious institutions, most of the ministry's activities are concerned with Jewish affairs. It controls Jewish life via three establishments: the ecclesiastical courts, the system of local religious councils, and the rabbinate, headed by two chief rabbis — one serving the Ashkenazic communities, one the Sephardic. Separate but equal, these two supreme officeholders do not always agree; clashes in the 1970s between the Ashkenazic and Sephardic chief rabbis approximated the pace and intensity of a world-championship tennis match as each contradicted the other's decisions on points of religious law,

ranging from the text of a new prayer book to the morality of Jews living in the occupied territories.

Whichever chief rabbi they follow, the Orthodox affirm that the Halakah — Jewish law — should be the law of Israel. The non-Orthodox, and indeed the non-Jewish minority in the electorate, are bound to disagree.

No Israeli would deny that the religious minority has power primarily because of its political clout. But to some extent, this power also depends on common consent. It is now accepted as axiomatic among the nonreligious majority that it was the Jewish faith that preserved the identity of the Jewish people during the centuries of dispersion. In consequence, the public is inclined to feel that religious sensitivities should be respected, although, on occasion, there have been angry denunciations of "coercion."

Some of the fiercest controversies between religious and nonreligious Israelis arise over the application of ancient religious law to people's private lives. One incident that aroused considerable wrath among the nonobservant, and much embarrassment among the pious, was the case of the *mamzerim* (the bastards) in 1971. A brother and sister, both serving in the Israeli Defense Forces, became engaged to Israeli Jews. Their mother had been married in Poland to a Jewish convert, but she had left him and emigrated to Israel with another man. It was only after she bore her new partner a son and a daughter that she obtained a divorce from her first husband and married the father of her children.

When the children applied to the rabbinical courts for marriage licenses, they were refused. According to religious law, children born to a married

woman and a man other than her husband are illegitimate and permitted to marry only other such illegitimates or converts to the Jewish faith. The decision outraged the public and stimulated demands that civil marriage be introduced in Israel.

The controversy continued for about a year, until it was defused by the application of subtle rabbinical casuistry, which determined that, since the first husband's conversion to Judaism was doubtful, the Polish marriage was invalid. The two young couples were allowed to marry, and the chief rabbi himself performed the ceremony. But the law was not changed. Because Orthodox rabbis will not solemnize marriages between Jews and non-Jews, those who want to wed outside the faith have to leave the country to do so; however, foreign marriage is accepted by the state as legally valid, and the children are considered legitimate. Divorce, too, remains in the hands of the rabbis, priests and Islamic divines: Only the rabbinical courts can grant divorces to Jews, only the Islamic religious courts to Muslims.

When the clerics prove intransigent, aggrieved individuals turn to the Supreme Court. A bizarre case, which came before the court in 1984, concerned the burial of Tereza Anghelovici, a Christian who had come to Israel from Rumania with her Jewish husband 20 years before. She lived her life as a loyal citizen of Israel, brought up her children as Jews and, when she died, was interred in a Jewish cemetery. Some time after her burial, the local senior rabbi was made aware of her origins and decided that since the dead woman was not Jewish, she had no right to lie in a Jewish burial ground. He insisted that her body be exhumed and

Demonstrators outside the prime minister's residence in Jerusalem protest the massacre in Beirut of some 800 Palestinian refugees by Lebanese Christian militiamen. The 1982 Israeli invasion of Lebanon provoked greater domestic opposition than any other war in Israel's history.

interred elsewhere. The Ministry of Health disagreed and, while the argument proceeded, some ultraorthodox Jews dug up and removed the dead woman's remains. The Supreme Court ruled that the body be returned to the original Jewish grave.

Even a seemingly uncontroversial subject, such as Daylight Savings Time, may raise hackles throughout the community. The economic, energy-saving advantages of turning clocks ahead in summertime are so substantial that the system has been adopted throughout the Western world. When Daylight Savings Time was introduced into Israel on an experimental basis in the summer of 1984, however, Orthodox Jews protested that it would encourage Israelis to desecrate the Sabbath: Public transportation and movies might start before sunset. One rabbi declared: "What are a few million — or even a few billion — dollars saved on energy compared to what we are losing in spiritual terms?" But cost cutting of this magnitude was not dismissed so lightly by the government, and the plan was formally adopted in 1985.

Yet rabbinical disputations and the scrupulous observance of religious law are worlds away from the concerns of many of the ordinary citizens. "When we lived in the United States," admitted a young Israeli couple who had spent three years studying in California, "we went to synagogue every Friday night as a way of identifying with the Jewish community. But here at home, we don't find a need for it. We are Israelis first, and we are part of a Jewish heritage. We know our Bible — it is our history and our culture. But we don't observe religious practices because we don't see them fitting in with modern life." Such views are typical of many members of the younger generation of Israelis, especially those who have lived or traveled in the West.

The synagogue may be the center of Jewish community life elsewhere, but in Israel it is solely a place for worship. Architecturally, too, Israeli synagogues are plain: Theirs is not a tradition of imposing façades and soaring spires. Most are small, simple and intimate houses of prayer. Jerusalem alone has some 800 synagogues, and most cater to tiny close-knit congregations from the same place of origin.

At sunset on Friday evening and early on Saturday morning, they are all operating at full strength, particularly in Mea Shearim and in the Old City. Humble rooms are full of worshippers, the Hasidim resplendent in their fur-trimmed hats and silk caftans. From street to narrow street in the Jewish Quarter of the Old City, the followers of dozens of different *rebbes* rend the air as they call upon their God. Elsewhere, Jews from Yemen, Iraq, Iran, Egypt, India and Ethiopia worship, each with distinctive liturgies, melodies and rituals evolved over centuries in their scattered communities.

Nowhere is the climate of traditional religious life in the Diaspora more carefully preserved than in the 500 state-subsidized yeshivoth. Yeshiva students, numbering some 50,000, are exempt from service in the Israeli Defense Forces on the ground that they are engaged in the spiritual rebuilding of Judaism after the ravages of the Holocaust. They claim that this function is no less vital to the future of Israel than the physical defense of the state. Some of these scholars will become rabbis, but after many years of study, most will live out their lives within the staunchly observant ultraorthodox communities, earning their keep by other means.

149

6

Within the milieu known to its denizens as the "yeshiva world," there has arisen a new, post-Six Day War phenomenon: the Yeshivoth for Penitents. Within these institutions, Jews from secular, nonobservant backgrounds strive to return to the orthodoxy of their ancestors. The schools offer short courses for young Jews coming from the Western world in search of Jewish inspiration, and for those who choose to stay longer they offer a new way of life. The first yeshiva of this type was founded by an American rabbi in 1967, at a time when many young American Jews were, like their non-Jewish contemporaries, protesting against the Vietnam War and rebelling against their affluent upbringing. For the generation who backpacked to remote parts to "find themselves," the idea of living in a yeshiva in Jerusalem was as exotic as sitting at the feet of an Indian guru in Benares. To the surprise of some, the Penitents movement, although still small, survived the 1960s and continues to grow. But whether its students are the scions of old Hasidic families or dropouts from American suburbia, yeshiva education caters to a minority within a minority.

For the bulk of the Israeli population, the source of Jewish education is the national school system. Parents may choose between three forms of education: secular state schools, state religious schools and the ultraorthodox Agudat Israel schools, which are outside the state system but receive some funding from the government. Some 70 percent of Jewish pupils attend the ordinary schools, 25 percent the state-run religious system and 5 percent the Agudat Israel institutions. Arab children are educated in a separate state-run system, study Arabic as their first language and receive instruction in Arabic history and culture.

All of the non-Arab schools in the state system include education in the values of Jewish culture. But while the secular schools use Biblical studies as a foundation for teaching history and archeology, the religious schools concentrate more heavily on religious law and ritual, devoting correspondingly less time to mathematics, sciences and other secular studies.

Judaism, as the religious education system emphasizes, is a way of life; so all-encompassing is the faith that the Hebrew language originally had no word for "religion" in the sense of a system of beliefs. Devout Jews follow an elaborately mapped out sequence of daily rituals. Birth, coming of age, marriage and death all have their prescribed customs and ceremonies, and even those who are not otherwise particularly observant will celebrate their weddings under the traditional canopy — marking the exchange of vows by smashing a glass — and later will have their infant sons ritually circumcised in accordance with ancient Jewish law.

But no other event in Jewish life is as important as the weekly day of rest. The fourth of the Ten Commandments enjoins the Jewish people to remember the Sabbath and keep it holy. "Six days shalt thou labor and do all thy work, but the seventh day is the Sabbath of the Lord thy God." Modern Israel works a frenetic six-day week, but on the seventh day the nation rests, and an almost-palpable peace prevails.

The holiday runs from sunset on Friday to Saturday evening, ending when the first stars can be seen in the sky. In preparation, nearly all of the Jewish shops and markets close soon after

An elderly man wearing an elaborate silver-threaded tallith, or prayer shawl, blows on the shofar — a ram's horn fitted with a reed. One of the oldest instruments known, the shofar is used on the High Holy Days.

THE FESTIVAL YEAR

Many festivals and holy days in the Jewish calendar are observed in Israel as both religious and secular holidays. They vary in mood, from the solemnity of Rosh Hashanah (New Year) and Yom Kippur (the Day of Atonement) to the happy gift-giving feast of Hanukkah.

One of the most joyous of the festivals is Sukkoth (right), which occurs over five days in September or October. The holiday takes its name from the makeshift shelters used by the Israelites during their 40-year sojourn in the wilderness after the Exodus from Egypt.

Families mark the feast at home by building huts that are topped with branches and decorated with fruits and flowers. And some Israelis make pilgrimages to Jerusalem to visit the giant community sukkah on Mount Zion and to pray at the Western Wall.

During Sukkoth, a crowd of men —
many with their heads totally covered
by talithim — prays before the Western
Wall in Jerusalem. Following a Biblical
injunction, each man carries a palm
branch, or lulab, as well as a sprig of
myrtle, a spray of willow and an ethrog — an ancient species of citrus.

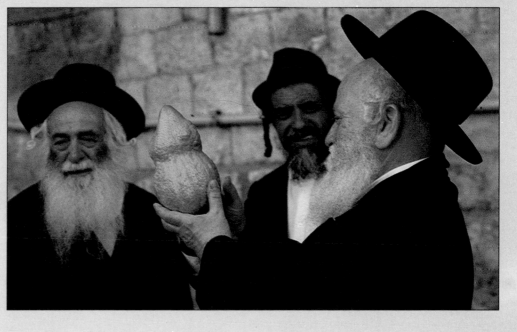

Three potential purchasers admire an
outsize ethrog. The fruit, which is
grown and bought for its ritual rather
than its edible value, symbolizes the agricultural aspects of Sukkoth, which is
celebrated worldwide at the time
of the harvest in ancient Palestine.

In the stony fields of the West Bank, south of Bethlehem, an Arab man and woman guide their mules past new homes for Jewish settlers. For some Israelis, moving to the West Bank is a symbolic act: a recovery of the Biblical lands of Samaria and Judaea. Others vigorously oppose the settlement.

noon on Friday. So does public transportation (although the privately owned taxis known as *sheruts* operate). The degrees of official Sabbath observance vary: In predominantly secular Haifa, buses continue to run, while in districts with substantial concentrations of Orthodox Jews, the period is marked more rigidly: Chains close streets to traffic and shop windows are dark. But everywhere, even in urban, cosmopolitan and sophisticated Tel Aviv, the hustle of the work week gives way to relaxation and tranquillity. In city, village and kibbutz, the Jews of Israel — observant and nonobservant alike — greet one another with *"Shabbath shalom"* — "a peaceful Sabbath."

But the peace is sometimes broken by those who claim to cherish the divinely ordained day of rest the most. From time to time, the peace and serenity of the Sabbath are broken as ultraorthodox Jews, the Haredim, demonstrate angrily and sometimes violently at the desecration of that sacred period by their less-religious compatriots. In such areas as Mea Shearim in Jerusalem, the time-honored rites of Sabbath observance — prayers in synagogues, ceremonial family meals, the recitation of blessings — are carried out in conjunction with a more contemporary ritual: attacking those citizens who choose to spend their Saturday in secular pursuits. Residents, young and old, will gather on the roads that bound their neighborhood to throw stones at the passing cars that disturb their Sabbath isolation. In the town of Petah Tikvah, a few miles from Tel Aviv, near-riots took place every Friday evening for several weeks as Haredim in large numbers held demonstrations against the opening of the new local movie theater.

In addition to the Sabbath, the calendar is punctuated by religious holidays, each with its rich accretion of symbolic acts and ceremonies. The year begins with the High Holy Days — the New Year festival of Rosh Hashanah and the solemn Day of Atonement, Yom Kippur, when the devout ask forgiveness for their sins. These are followed by various major and minor festivals, such as Hanukkah — the midwinter Festival of Lights, commemorating the struggles of ancient Jewish patriots against Roman oppression — and Shabuoth, in the late spring, which celebrates the revelation of the Ten Commandments to Moses on Mount Sinai.

In Israel, nonreligious Jews also observe some of these ancient festivals and anniversaries, though not necessarily in the traditional forms. This is particularly evident in the kibbutzim.

The earliest kibbutz members — all socialists — rejected everything to do with religion. While the secular kibbutzim remain in the majority, some collectives were founded by observant Jews. The leaders of the movement, however opposed to religious rituals, nevertheless recognized that their history was Jewish history, that their holidays were the Jewish Holy Days and that Saturday was their Sabbath.

As a result, they tried to infuse all the old institutions with new content. In most kibbutzim today, the Sabbath is not merely a respite from work but a day devoted to the refreshment of the spirit — including concerts, plays, lectures, discussions. On the festival of Passover, Jewish families participate in a Seder — a ritual meal to commemorate the Israelites' exodus from Egypt and their release from slavery — and the extended family of the kibbutz also holds its own communal feast. In place of the texts that are traditionally read as

part of the Seder service, new readings have been created, which relate Biblical struggles for freedom to more recent events. In all of these, the Nazi Holocaust figures prominently, as does the oppression of the Soviet Jews.

Throughout the Jewish world, the autumn harvest festival of Sukkoth, or Feast of Tabernacles, is observed with synagogue services. In most kibbutzim, however, it is celebrated in the open air, with pageants, entertainment, and displays of the community's own freshly harvested produce and newest manufactured goods: Piles of oranges and avocados share the place of honor with microchips.

Even in the cities, new expressions have been given to religious occasions. Thousands of Israelis have revived the ancient practice of a Sukkoth pilgrimage to Jerusalem; others enjoy a much-younger tradition — a wine-tasting festival, celebrating the new vintage from Israel's oldest vineyards, founded by Baron Edmond de Rothschild in 1882.

Purim — commemorating the salvation of the Jews in Persia when the wiles of Queen Esther thwarted a wicked minister's designs against them — has always been one of the most joyous days of the Jewish calendar, celebrated by the reading of the Book of Esther in synagogues and parties for children at home. In Israel today, it is a national festival, a time of carnivals, costume parades and public entertainment — in short, an Israeli answer to Mardi Gras.

Despite their enthusiastic participation in Purim parades and Passover Seders, most Israelis have abandoned the traditional Jewish lifestyle. In the coastal towns, many more people enjoy the day of rest on the beaches than in the synagogues. Large crowds attend

6

soccer matches and other sports events.

But some observers believe that the tide is turning and religion is becoming increasingly significant in Israeli life. The Sephardic members of the population have tended to cling more tenaciously to Jewish observance than have their Ashkenazic coreligionists. Coming mainly from North Africa and the Middle East, where piety and poverty tended to go hand in hand, the Sephardic immigrants of the 1950s were a disadvantaged group. Struggling with problems of cultural assimilation and economic deprivation, they had little opportunity to exercise the influence their numbers would justify. In the 1970s, however, the government of Prime Minister Menachem Begin made political appointments that gave the Sephardim a greater share of political power. In 1984, the formation of a separate Sephardic religious party — the Shas — broke the Ashkenazim's monopoly of the religious establishment. As the Sephardim's influence increased, so did their assertiveness: Sephardic loyalty to traditional Jewish practices and values now has a greater impact than ever before.

Perhaps in response to these influences, many Ashkenazim are also beginning to reassess the role of Judaism in their lives. The Six Day and Yom Kippur wars, and the increasing hostility of the outside world to Israel in its unsympathetic role as an occupying power, have driven people to look inward for historical and Biblical roots.

Israel today, therefore, may conceivably be more Jewish than at any other time in its short history. Such, however, is not the view of the very small and electorally insignificant minority of ultraorthodox. Nothing will satisfy them short of a society based exclusively on

the Jewish law — and many of them are prepared to use violence in order to achieve that end.

In his final Independence Day address as president in 1983, Yitzhak Navon warned of the dangers that could arise from all forms of religious and political intolerance. "The question is not if there will be arguments among us, but if we will know how to conduct them," he said. "The question has become a central factor in our lives, in our ability to sustain democracy and, quite simply, to live with each other."

But contentiousness is not confined simply to the theological sphere. Political issues are also the subject of fierce debate — and none more so than Israel's relations with the Arabs. Indeed, there was bitter internal controversy as a consequence of the government's inability to bring the war in Lebanon to a swift conclusion.

According to the government, the sole object of the invasion of Lebanon — named Operation *Peace for Galilee* — was to clear the deployment of PLO arms and men away from Israel's northern border, to which they presented a continuing and mounting threat. At first, most Israelis supported the move, but opinion divided dramatically when the invasion force went on to bombard the PLO strongholds in the city of Beirut, claiming that this was a military necessity if they were to bring the operation to a successful end.

In fact, the PLO eventually agreed to leave the Lebanese capital, but only after the city had been severely bombarded. Mediators, such as U.S. Special Envoy Philip Habib, had made earlier attempts to persuade the PLO to leave Beirut, but to no avail. The relief caused by the PLO departure was soon

overshadowed by the shocking news that some 800 PLO fighters and Palestinian refugees had been massacred by the Lebanese Phalangists — right-wing Christian militia forces. An estimated 350,000 Israelis — nearly a tenth of the country's population — took to the streets in protest.

However, there were many Israelis, especially among the Sephardic community, who not only applauded the tough line in Lebanon but also saw the antiwar protestors as virtual traitors. The ferment culminated in an act of political violence in February of 1983, when an assailant hurled a hand grenade into a crowd of antigovernment demonstrators who were gathered outside the prime minister's office in Jerusalem, killing a 33-year-old reserve paratrooper who had fought in both the Six Day and Yom Kippur wars.

The attack shocked the people into realizing the consequences of Israel's internal dissension. Interior Minister Joseph Burg called it "the gravest of warnings" for the whole Israeli nation. "We must remember," declared President Yitzhak Navon, "that we are one people, with one common destiny, and if, God forbid, our existence should be threatened, we are all in the same boat."

Peace protestors are not the only ones to have suffered at the hands of violent extremists. In 1984, Israelis were shocked to learn of an underground Jewish terrorist group that had been mounting attacks against Arabs living in the territories occupied by Israel during the Six Day War. The victims included two West Bank mayors, both of whom were maimed in car-bomb explosions, and three students, killed in a machine-gun attack on the Islamic College in Hebron.

Israelis were disturbed to find that

154

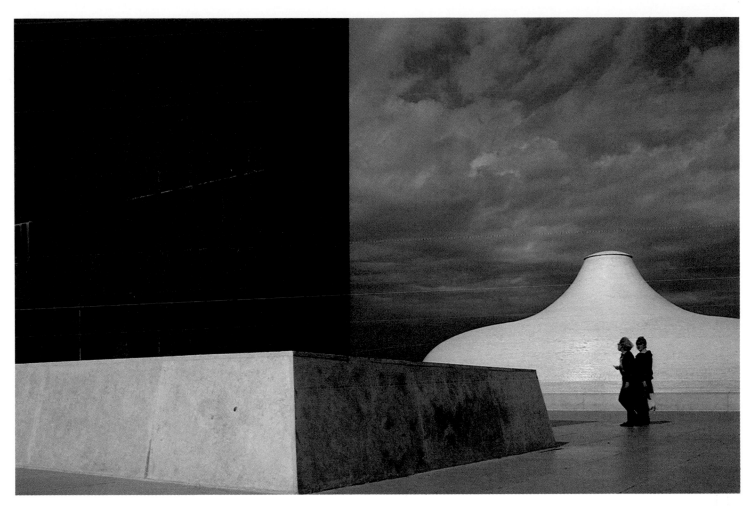

such an organization existed at all; they were more disturbed by the list of those accused of taking part. Not all were fringe fanatics. Some were prominent members of Gush Emunim (Bloc of the Faithful), the nationalist religious movement spearheading Jewish settlement on the West Bank. Initially, the Gush Emunim community itself was shocked by the revelation.

Rabbi Moshe Levinger, a spiritual leader of the activists, infuriated most Israelis by claiming that his followers had been forced to take the law into their own hands because of the government's failure to safeguard the West Bank settlements against the PLO. "The arrested," he said, "will yet go down in history as dear boys who worked for the state at a time when it did not do enough on their behalf." Most Israelis rejected this out of hand. In a poll conducted by the Tel Aviv daily *Ha'aretz*, 60 percent of those questioned said that the anti-Arab violence was unjustified, though 32 percent felt that it was "totally justified" or had "a certain justification."

For many Israeli citizens, the problem in the occupied territories is part of the much broader question of how to live in peace. They wonder how Israel's future relations with the Palestinians are to be shaped. Former Foreign Minister Abba Eban has said, "When you think of this situation in the light of Jewish history and the struggle of the Jews for equality of rights and status, the paradox becomes agonizing."

But the paradox is recognized, and the fact that it is debated so widely and with such passion is itself a hopeful sign for the future. Indeed, if it can resolve the political and spiritual contradictions that rend it, Israel may yet realize the high hopes of its founders.

"If I am asked to sum up the whole sense of our purpose as a people and of our state," declared Ben-Gurion, "it is that we shall achieve our aims of peace, justice and the brotherhood of man, not by homily and preaching, but by being ourselves an example in our lives, our government and our conduct. And this we shall achieve only through the alliance of the pioneers of labor and the men of spirit." ☐

ACKNOWLEDGMENTS

The index for this book was prepared by Vicki Robinson. For their help in the preparation of this volume, the editors wish to thank the following people and institutions: Mahmoud Abu-Ragabah, Dhahiriya, West Bank; Ben-Gurion University of the Negev, Beersheba, Israel; David Ben-Rafael, Embassy of Israel, London; Mike Brown, London; Alex Burke, Bromley, Kent, England; Richard Cleave, Jerusalem; Jane Curry, London; Mandy Davis, Britain and Israel Public Affairs Committee (BIPAC), London; Dorit Farkash, Kiryat Yam, Israel; Neyla Freeman, London; Benjamin Gil, Ben-Gurion University Foundation, London; Sue Haas, BIPAC, London; Shoshan Haim, Israel Ports Authority, Ashdod, Israel; Zelda Harris, Committee of Concerned Citizens, Netanya, Israel; Rona Hart, Committee of Concerned Citizens, Tel Aviv; Klaus-Otto Hundt, Warwick, England; Kibbutz Ma'Agan Michael, Ma'Agan Michael, Israel; Tommy Lamm, London; Linda Levine, BIPAC, Tel Aviv; Nigel Lillicrap, London; Janet McKenzie, London; Jane Moonman, BIPAC, London; Anton Neumann, BIPAC, London; Robin Olson, London; Matsliah Rafi, Ministry of Tourism, Beersheba, Israel; Deborah Richardson, BIPAC, London; Jonathon Riley-Smith, Egham, Surrey; Faye Schlinsky, Ministry of Tourism, Jerusalem; Barry Shenker, BIPAC, London; Michelle Shinegold, BIPAC, London; Pearl Silver, Jerusalem; Angela Silverman, BIPAC, London; Deborah Thompson, London; The Wiener Library, London.

BIBLIOGRAPHY

BOOKS

Aamiry, M. A., *Jerusalem: Arab Origin and Heritage*. London: Longman, 1978.

Avi-Yonah, Michael, *The Holy Land*. London: Thames and Hudson, 1972.

Baedeker's Israel. Basingstoke, England: Automobile Association, 1983.

Banks, Lynn Reid, *Letters to My Israeli Sons*. London: W. H. Allen, 1979.

Becker, Jillian, *The PLO*. London: Weidenfeld & Nicolson, 1984.

Bellow, Saul, *To Jerusalem and Back*. London: Martin Secker & Warburg, 1976.

Ben-Gurion, David, ed., *The Jews in Their Land*. London: Aldus Books, 1966.

Ben-Rafael, Eliezer, *The Emergence of Ethnicity: Cultural Groups and Social Conflict in Israel*. Westport, Connecticut: Greenwood Press, 1982.

Bermant, Chaim:
Israel. London: Thames and Hudson, 1967.
The Jews. London: Weidenfeld & Nicolson, 1977.

Capa, Cornell, *Jerusalem: City of Mankind*. London: Harrap, 1974.

Chapman, Alex, *Begin's Israel, Mubarak's Egypt*. London: W. H. Allen, 1983.

Chomsky, Noam, *The Fateful Triangle*. London: Pluto Press, 1983.

Davis, Moshe, and Isaac Levy, *All about Israel*. London: Jewish National Fund, 1973.

Dayan, Moshe, *Living with the Bible*. London: Weidenfeld & Nicolson, 1978.

Dicks, Brian, *The Israelis: How They Live and Work*. London: David & Charles, 1975.

Eban, Abba:
My Country: The Story of Modern Israel. London: Weidenfeld & Nicolson, 1972.
The New Diplomacy. London: Weidenfeld & Nicolson, 1983.

Elon, Amos, *The Israelis*. London: Penguin Books, 1983.

Fine, Leon, *Will the Real Israel Please Stand Up?* Givatayim, Israel: Pelmas/Massada, 1980.

Frankel, William, *Israel Observed*. London: Thames and Hudson, 1980.

Gilmour, David, *Dispossessed*. London: Sidgwick & Jackson, 1980.

Good News Bible. London: Collins/Fount Bible Society, 1978.

Guiladi, Yael, *One Jerusalem*. Jerusalem: Keter Publishing House, 1983.

Herzog, Chaim, *The Arab-Israeli Wars*. London: Arms and Armour Press, 1982.

Hollis, Christopher, and Ronald Brownrigg, *Holy Places*. New York: Frederick A. Praeger, 1969.

Holy Bible in the King James Version. Oxford, England: Oxford University Press, 1974.

Horowitz, David, *The Economics of Israel*. London: Pergamon Press, 1967.

Isaac, Rael Jean, *Party and Politics in Israel*. New York: Longman, 1981.

Israel Pocket Library:
Archaeology. Jerusalem: Keter Publishing House, 1974.
Education and Science. Jerusalem: Keter Publishing House, 1974.
History. Jerusalem: Keter Publishing House, 1973.
Immigration and Settlement. Jerusalem: Keter Publishing House, 1973.
Geography. Jerusalem: Keter Publishing House, 1973.

Johnson, Paul, *Civilizations of the Holy Land*. London: Weidenfeld & Nicolson, 1979.

Katz, Eliahu, and Michael Gurevitch, *The Secularization of Leisure: Culture and Communication in Israel*. London: Faber & Faber, 1976.

Kaufman, Gerald, *To Build the Promised Land*. London: Weidenfeld & Nicolson, 1973.

Kedourie, Elie, ed., *The Jewish World*. London: Thames and Hudson, 1979.

Kimche, Jon, *The Second Arab Awakening*. London: Thames and Hudson, 1970.

Kollek, Teddy, and Moshe Pearlman, *Jerusalem: Sacred City of Mankind*. London: Weidenfeld & Nicolson, 1974.

Laffin, John:
The Arab Mind. London: Cassell, 1979.
The Israeli Mind. London: Cassell, 1979.

Landay, Jerry M., and the Editors of Newsweek Book Division, *Dome of the Rock*. New York: Newsweek, 1972.

Lange, Nicholas de, *Atlas of the Jewish World*. Oxford, England: Phaidon, 1984.

Lind, Jakov, *The Trip to Jerusalem*. London: Jonathan Cape, 1974.

Meir, Golda, *My Life*. London: Futura, 1982.

Mikes, George, *The Prophet Motive: Israel Today and Tomorrow*. London: Penguin Books, 1971.

Naamani, Israel T., *Israel*. London: Pall Mall Press, 1972.

Orni, Efraim, and Elisha Efrat, *Geography of Israel.* Jerusalem: Israel Universities Press, 1976.

Oz, Amos, *In the Land of Israel.* London: Flamingo, 1983.

Peretz, Don, *The Government and Politics of Israel.* Boulder, Colorado: Westview Press, 1979.

Perowne, Stewart, *Jerusalem & Bethlehem.* London: Phoenix House, 1965.

Prittie, Terence, *Whose Jerusalem?* London: Frederick Muller, 1981.

Rein, Natalie, *Daughters of Rachel: Women in Israel.* New York: Penguin Books, 1980.

Rosenblatt, Roger, *Children of War.* London: New English Library, 1984.

Sachar, Howard M., *A History of Israel.* Oxford, England: Basil Blackwell, 1977.

Silver, Eric, *Begin: A Biography.* London: Weidenfeld & Nicolson, 1984.

Statistical Abstract of Israel. No. 35. Jerusalem: Central Bureau of Statistics, 1984.

Sykes, Christopher, *Cross Roads to Israel.* London: Collins, 1965.

Thubron, Colin, and the Editors of Time-Life Books, *Jerusalem* (The Great Cities series). Amsterdam: Time-Life Books, 1976.

Time-Life Books, Editors of, *The Israelites* (The Emergence of Man series). New York: Time-Life Books, 1975.

Weizman, Ezer, *The Battle for Peace.* Toronto: Bantam Books, 1981.

Wilson, Rodney, *The Economies of the Middle East.* London: Macmillan, 1979.

Zohar, Danah, *Israel.* London: Macdonald Educational, 1977.

Zureik, Elia T., *The Palestinians in Israel.* London: Routledge & Kegan Paul, 1979.

PERIODICALS

"Chief Rabbis in Conflict." *Jewish Chronicle,* September 7, 1984.

"God on Their Side." *Observer Magazine,* July 22, 1984.

Jerusalem Post Magazine:
   "Dangerous Inroads." May 3, 1985.
   "The Names Game." June 22, 1984.

"Mimouna." *The Jerusalem Post Supplement,* April 11, 1985.

Newsweek:
   "An American Presence." June 4, 1984.
   "The Troubled Soul of Israel." October 4, 1982.

Plascov, Avi, "A Palestinian State? Examining the Alternatives." *Adelphi Papers* (London: The International Institute for Strategic Studies), spring 1981.

Time:
   "Children of War." January 11, 1982.
   "The Verdict Is Guilty." February 21, 1983.
   "What Next for Israel?" July 9, 1984.

"You're in the Army Now." *She,* February 1985.

PICTURE CREDITS

Credits from left to right are separated by semicolons, from top to bottom by dashes.

Cover: Hans Wiesenhofer, Vienna. Front endpaper: Map by Roger Stewart, London. Back endpaper: Digitized map by Creative Data, London.

1, 2: © Flag Research Center, Winchester, Massachusetts. 6-9: Hans Wiesenhofer, Vienna. 10: Map by Creative Data, London. 10,11: Hans Wiesenhofer, Vienna. 12: Chart by Mechanicals 4 Designers, Annandale, Virginia. 12-19: Hans Wiesenhofer, Vienna. 20: Hans Wiesenhofer, Vienna; Richard Nowitz, Jerusalem — Hans Wiesenhofer (4). 21: Hans Wiesenhofer, Vienna; Orde Eliason, London; Hans Wiesenhofer, Vienna (7). 23: David Rubinger, Jerusalem. 24, 25: Digitized images by Creative Data, London. 26, 27: Hans Wiesenhofer, Vienna. 28: Klaus-Otto Hundt, Warwick, England. 29-51: Hans Wiesenhofer, Vienna. 52: Courtesy of Staats- und Universitätsbibliothek, Hamburg, photo BPCC/Aldus Archive, London. 53: Courtesy of the Rothschild Miscellany from the Israel Museum, Jerusalem. 54: Illumination from 13th-century Haggadah, BPCC/Aldus Archive, London. 55: Jane Taylor from Sonia Halliday Photographs, Weston Turville, England. 56: Illumination from a French history by William of Tyre, BPCC/Aldus Archive, London. 57: Sonia Halliday Photographs, Weston Turville, England. 58: *The Judgment of Solomon,* a 13th-century miniature from a Hebrew manuscript, courtesy the British Library, London (Add. Ms. 11639 F. 518R), photo BPCC/Aldus Archive, London; 12th-century manuscript, courtesy of the Armenian Cathedral Library, Jerusalem, photo Sonia Halliday Photographs, Weston Turville, England; from *Underground Jerusalem* by Charles Warren, pub. Richard Bentley and Son, London, 1876. 59: *Naphtali* by Marc Chagall, © ADAGP, 1985, photo Sonia Halliday/Laura Lushington from Sonia Halliday Photographs, Weston Turville, England; David Rubinger, Jerusalem (3). 60-63: BPCC/Aldus Archive, London. 65: Popperfoto, London. 66: BPCC/Aldus Archive, London. 67: David Rubinger, Jerusalem. 68-76: Hans Wiesenhofer, Vienna. 77: David Rubinger, Jerusalem. 79-83: Hans Wiesenhofer, Vienna. 84: Digitized image by Creative Data, London. 85: Amos Schliack from Focus, Hamburg. 86, 87: Michael Freeman, London; Hans Wiesenhofer, Vienna. 88: Hans Wiesenhofer, Vienna. 89: Mark Karras, London. 90: Hans Wiesenhofer, Vienna. 91: Reg Wilson, London. 92, 93: Digitized image by Creative Data, London; Hans Wiesenhofer, Vienna. 94-97: Hans Wiesenhofer, Vienna. 98, 99: Hans Wiesenhofer, Vienna; David Rubinger, Jerusalem. 100-103: Hans Wiesenhofer, Vienna. 104, 105: Amos Schliack from Focus, Hamburg. 106, 107: Hans Wiesenhofer, Vienna. 108: Laura Lushington from Sonia Halliday Photographs, Weston Turville, England. 109-117: Hans Wiesenhofer, Vienna. 118: Richard Nowitz, Jerusalem. 121-125: Hans Wiesenhofer, Vienna. 126, 127: Richard Nowitz, Jerusalem. 128-131: Hans Wiesenhofer, Vienna. 133: David Rubinger, Jerusalem. 134, 135: Hans Wiesenhofer, Vienna. 136, 137: Richard Nowitz, Jerusalem — Hans Wiesenhofer, Vienna (2). 138-143: Hans Wiesenhofer, Vienna. 145: David Rubinger, Jerusalem. 146, 147: Amos Schliack from Focus, Hamburg. 149: David Rubinger, Jerusalem. 150: Orde Eliason, London. 151: Richard Nowitz, Jerusalem. 152-155: Hans Wiesenhofer, Vienna.

INDEX

Time-Life Books Inc. offers a wide range of fine recordings, including a *Rock 'n' Roll Era* series. For subscription information, call 1-800-621-7026, or write TIME-LIFE MUSIC, P.O. Box C-32068, Richmond, Virginia 23261-2068.

SYRIA

DEMILITARIZED
ZONE

LEBANON

GOLAN
HEIGHTS

SEA OF
GALILEE

Safad

Tiberias

Nazareth

Nahariyya

Acre

BAY OF
HAIFA

Haifa

Caesarea

Hadera

Netanya

Herzliyya

Tel Aviv-Jaffa

Petah Tikvah

Rishon le Zion

Rehovot

Nablus

WEST
BANK

Jericho

Jerusalem

Qumran

Bethlehem

Hebron

En Gedi

DEAD
SEA

Ashdod

Ashkelon

Kiryat Gat

Sederot

Gaza

GAZA STRIP

MEDITERRANEAN SEA